True DISCIPLE

ROD NICHOLS

Publishing Coordinator – Sharon Kizziah-Holmes
Cover Design – Jaycee DeLorenzo

Paperback-Press
an imprint of A & S Publishing
A & S Holmes, Inc.

ISBN -13: 978-1-951772-18-5

ACKNOWLEDGMENTS

I first want to thank Jesus for dying on the cross for my salvation. I am eternally grateful.

Second, I'd like to thank God for the writing abilities that He blessed me with and for the amazing, life changing experiences on the path to becoming a true disciple.

Third, is a big THANK YOU to Karen, my wife, for her love, patience with me on my journey, and her many hours of editing on this manuscript.

Fourth, I want to thank Tim Johnson, my spiritual mentor, who is mentioned several times in the book. Without his friendship and teaching, I would not be the true disciple I am today.

Last, but not least, I'd like to thank Sharon Kizziah-Holmes at Paperback Press for the professional layout and Jaycee DeLorenzo for the fantastic cover design.

CONTENTS

INTRODUCTION

"When you produce much fruit, you are my true disciples. This brings great glory to my Father."
John 15:8 NLT]

Jesus called those who followed him, disciples. A disciple is a student, a learner, an imitator of their teacher. Those of us who call ourselves followers of Jesus or Christians, should be imitators of him. We should look like, act like, and do what he did. In fact, Jesus told his disciples that because he was going to heaven, they would do even greater things than he did. That's amazing, since he healed, delivered, raised the dead, turned water into wine, fed 10,000 + people with a few fish and loaves, and walked on water. Yet, that's what He told the disciples and since he was fully God and God cannot lie, that must be the truth. Yet, we see very little of that in our western culture.

Jesus is Returning Soon!

Time is running out and Jesus will return soon. There are many millions of people on a path to eternal torment in hell, because there are so few true disciples. In this book I tell my story of becoming a true disciple of Jesus Christ and at the same time teach the difference between true disciples and those sitting in comfy chairs, enjoying great worship music, and listening to a good message a few Sundays each month.

God is calling His children to get out from behind the comfort of the church walls. He wants us to go into the world and tell people about the Kingdom of God and what Jesus has done in our lives. He wants us to lead people to the saving grace of Jesus (not just invite them to church so the professionals can lead them to the Lord). Then, we are to help them become true disciples, who will go and do the same.

Is God Calling You?

As the first disciples found, that following Jesus as a true disciple can be messy and dangerous. In this book I hope to help you count the costs before you make a life altering decision. The good news is that, as we see in the Bible, once the disciples made the decision to follow Jesus, their lives were never the same and they impacted millions. of people, including you and me. It's possible that God is calling you to do the same.

Imagine all the lives you could impact if you were a sold-out follower of Jesus, a true disciple? In fact, can you imagine what our world would be like if all Christians were true disciples? Wow, it would be a great place to live and perhaps a little more like heaven.

What's exciting is that it could happen, and it starts with us. Become a true disciple and impact your part of the world. Then make more true disciples who will impact their part of the world. Our communities will change. Our cities will improve. Our country will once again be great - in God's eyes. All because you became a true disciple!

CHAPTER ONE

†

BEGINNING

Y ou're probably thinking that I'm going back to
Genesis and the beginning of our world, but I'm
not. I'm going back to my beginning to start telling
you my story of becoming a true disciple of Jesus Christ.

Over the last two decades the Lord has allowed me to
lead the men's ministry at a large church, help plant two
churches, operate a traveling teaching ministry, write a
couple books, teach and preach the gospel, make disciples,
and help launch a national ministry for men. Through those
years, He has taught me to be a true disciple of Jesus
Christ. However, it wasn't always that way.

I grew up in a good middle-class home in Denver,
Colorado from around 1960 to 1973. My Dad worked in an
office and Mom stayed home with my brother and me. We
lived across the street from a Presbyterian church (my
Mom had Presbyterian background and my parents had
been married in a Presbyterian church), so that was where
we attended nearly every Sunday morning.

Sunday mornings were the worst. In fact, I have vivid
memories of hiding under the blankets in my bed, hoping

they would forget me, so I didn't have to go to church. They never did. Mom would chide me until I got up and put on my Sunday best for church. We would then march across the street and in to the little sanctuary. It was a solemn event – children needed to be quiet and even the adults were so quiet, you could have heard a pin drop (I'm sure that if that had happened, someone would have been in big trouble). A gray-haired church lady played the organ as we entered and sat in a hard wood pew (there weren't any cushy chairs back then).

Sunday's Were the Worst!

Once the service started, we would suffer through one hymn, which we stood to sing from a hymnal, an offertory piece on the organ or by the small choir (which always featured a big voice soprano woman belting it out above the rest), and a short, boring message from the minister. Fidgeting was not allowed and quickly, but quietly reprimanded by parents. Exactly one hour (which seemed like at least five hours) after it started the minister would speak the benediction and we would file out to the fellowship hall for coffee, punch and cookies (the only good part of church for me).

The Glory of God?

Back then, everyone smoked, so if I had had any idea about the glory of God, I might have thought that the glory had descended on the fellowship hall. Everyone would stand around gossiping about so in so or talking about how the service was too long, the music was too loud, the coffee wasn't hot enough and then we all went home to our lives.

My home didn't have a Bible that we ever read, and I don't remember ever praying at meals, except maybe on Thanksgiving and Easter. During those days in church, I heard all the Bible stories – Adam and Eve, Noah, Abraham, Isaac, Jacob, Samson, David and Goliath, and of course Jesus. I remember celebrating advent at Christmas – lighting the candles and opening the doors in the advent calendar (ours didn't have little chocolates in them, like some do today). I knew all about Mary and Joseph, Jesus being born in a manger, and then becoming a teacher. Unfortunately, I never quite got that I needed him as my Savior or I should make him Lord over my life. After-all, I was born in America, went to church every Sunday, gave my tithe (when I got older and was working), and hadn't committed any major sins (murder, adultery, and so on), obviously I was going to heaven.

Devil in Disguise

During these years of being a good church boy, I was more of a devil in my real life. My idea of the way things should go was my way or the highway. I organized the neighborhood kids into teams for sports, capture the flag, war games, and other activities. If any of them objected, I would yell them down. Yes, I had an anger problem. It led to many arguments, fights and some damaged friendships that never quite recovered. Unfortunately, I carried that anger issue into my adult life. More on that later.

From a young age I played sports. Baseball was my favorite sport and during the summer of my 16th year I made friends with a guy on my team. He introduced me to the thrilling adventure of shoplifting. He was quite an artist and I was an excellent disciple. We would go together, and I would watch the master at work. Soon, I was out on my own – stealing cassette tapes, golf gloves, and various other smaller items.

Wanting to impress the master, I started stealing larger items, which took some skill. Then one day, I was slipping something into my pants when a large hand grabbed my arm and began dragging me to an upper office where I stood face to face with the store manager and a police officer. I was mortified and couldn't stop crying. I was then led out of the store and into a waiting police car. The officer drove to my house, picked up my mom and took us both back to the store. Sitting in front of the manager, police officer, and my mom, I felt so much guilt and shame. I answered some questions with a quivering voice and tears flowing down my face and received my first recognizable blessing from God – they didn't charge me. I now understand that this was God protecting me, because He wanted to use me in the future.

Oh, Those College Years

After High School, I left Denver to attend college in Tacoma, WA at the University of Puget Sound (UPS). There I discovered the freedom of being on my own and making my own decisions. I also discovered partying and alcohol. We used to joke that at UPS we had our own special calendar – Monday, Friday, Saturday, Monday, Friday, Saturday, Sunday. Unless you were a science major (which I definitely was not), you didn't have classes on Wednesday, so Tuesday was like Friday, another party night, and then you had Wednesday to recover from the hangover. I was in a fraternity and so on Tuesday, Friday, and Saturday we had keggers and other parties that always included massive amounts of alcohol.

During my freshman year of college in 1973, something happened that rocked my little church world. Prior to leaving for college, I had made a financial commitment to the church to tithe. Well, about 2 months into my freshman year, I received a letter saying that because I had not met my financial commitment, I was no longer a member of the church. Here I was a poor, struggling college student, with no income and the church had kicked me out. I remember being so angry that I tore the letter into pieces so tiny that my fingers began to hurt. I then hurled them into the trash can and swore that I would never set foot in a church again, except for a wedding or funeral (I stood firm on that vow for 22 years – more on that later).

It was also during my freshman year that I discovered true Christianity. My first girlfriend was a Christian, which was cool, because I was too (or so I thought). She invited me to a campus meeting of Christians and primarily because I was interested in her, I went. WOW! These people were freaks – there was loud music, which was kind of cool, but they were raising their hands, swaying around like they were drunk (but they weren't), and speaking in a weird language. I ran out of the room and soon after, dumped the girl. I later realized that this was one of God's first attempts to pull me fully into the Kingdom, but I wasn't ready.

An Angry Young Man

College was a time when my anger issues escalated. I remember one time studying in my room and a drunk guy came up and threw water on me. I chased him down the hall, leaped down a flight of stairs and slammed him into a wall. I'm thankful that some other guys pulled me off the guy, as I was in a state of rage. Again, as in my younger days, I became known for my anger and it damaged some relationships.

During my senior year in college, I asked my second girlfriend to marry me and a week after graduation we were married in a big Catholic church. Yes, she was a Catholic, although she, like me, didn't really attend church anymore.

The church wedding was really for her parents and I had to spend a couple of sessions with the Priest to be deemed worthy to be married in the church. After the wedding, we went to Las Vegas for our honeymoon.

A week after that, I started my first corporate job. I worked hard for five years, won numerous awards and was promoted twice. I found success to be exhilarating, but the long hours and stress were damaging my marriage. Stress was also a trigger for my anger issue. My tongue was often used to whip my wife into my way of thinking and when stress escalated, damage to walls, doors, and other items was usually the result.

In 1983, I decided to leave the corporate world to become an entrepreneur and during those early years, my work addiction intensified. I would leave home early and return late. My wife had no real interest in my business world (even though I invited her to come see my office, retail store, and attend events) and she seemed to tolerate the long hours. We had a beautiful home and a new daughter, which monopolized my wife's attention. Instead of focusing on making my marriage work, I poured myself deeper into work, seeking attention, recognition, and wealth.

Softball and Drinking

When I wasn't working, I was playing competitive softball. We played several games each week and almost every weekend included an out of town tournament. Accompanying softball was always a lot of drinking. My wife accompanied me to a few of the games and some tournaments, but often I went alone. Success in sports brought attention and at times recognition in the form of trophies, but I still longed for some kind of deeper relationship.

About that time, I met a woman who had started a business that year as well. It started innocently enough as a business relationship. She and I both served on the board of a business association and met in a trade show booth. Our businesses were complimentary, so we began working together. There was some attraction, but we became supportive friends and continued a professional business relationship for the next two years.

As part of my business, I conducted a networking breakfast once a month. My friend was always at the breakfasts, networking for her business and learning more about sales and marketing from me and other speakers.

On a beautiful breakfast day in April, she arrived looking as if she had been crying. It had been several months since I had seen her. I asked if she was okay and she just nodded. I could feel her pain and approached her later to see if she would share what was wrong. She said she would rather not talk there, so I invited her to lunch to learn more about what was going on. At that lunch, I discovered that she was very unhappy and separating from her husband. I too was struggling in my marriage and so we compared notes for three hours and then revealed attraction for each other.

Pandora's Box

With Pandora's box open, we both left our spouses and moved in together. Before you judge us, remember that neither of us were saved and that Jesus said that he or she who is without sin can cast the first stone. By the way, the woman is now my wife and as of the writing of this book, Karen and I have been together for 35 years, married for nearly 32. We have conducted marriage conferences and counseled many couples, based on our mistakes and what we've learned. What the enemy meant for evil, God has turned into something very good.

By now you're probably wondering what all this has to do with being a true disciple. I will get into that in substance, later in the book. For now, just keep in mind that nearly everyone had a worldly life prior to making the decision to follow Jesus and become his disciple, including me. Peter was a fisherman, Matthew was a tax collector, Simon was a zealot, and Paul was a Jewish teacher and Christian hater. They too had their years of sin, which then made their conversion even more glorious and that's where I'm going, so stick with me.

Karen and I lived together for three years and then decided we should probably get married. This was her third marriage and my second. At the small backyard wedding, the justice of the peace (who was upset, because we were running late) told us that most second and third marriages don't make it, but he hoped we would. Wow! Cursed right out of the gate.

That Was a Crazy Time!

The first ten years were tumultuous, to say the least. My anger issues (and hers) were triggered often resulting in furious fights. I remember numerous occasions where we screamed obscenities at each other from different parts of the room or the landing of our apartment to the parking lot below. Many times, I left and screeched out of the parking lot, totally out of control, and fumed for hours, before returning.

We were juggling our five children (Karen had four and I had one) and trying to blend them in the middle of all the stress and conflict. Our first place was a small two-bedroom apartment with one bedroom dedicated to our office (as we both still had businesses that produced our only income). We had a couch, bed, dresser, and office furniture. Every other weekend the children stayed over (all five lived with our former spouses). They slept on the living room floor in sleeping bags and we ate off cardboard boxes.

After a nasty divorce battle, involving a blood thirsty attorney, I was required to pay more per month in child support than I was making. An ugly bankruptcy followed, which included repossession of my car. I remember that day like it was yesterday (yet it was over thirty years ago).

As I sat in our small, nearly empty apartment watching them repossess my car, I had my first and only thoughts of suicide. I thought about shooting myself but didn't have a gun. Then I thought I could take a bunch of pills, but didn't have any, nor did I have any money to buy them. Finally, I thought I could jump off the Narrows Bridge, but I was too afraid of heights. It's funny when I talk about it now, but I was serious as a heart attack back then. What stopped me from going down that path and finding a way, was a still small voice inside me that said I had more to do. Although I didn't recognize it at the time, it was the first time I heard the voice of God.

The Money Machine

Within a couple weeks of that day, I was forced to close my business and started hunting for a job. My parents loaned me some money (which is really embarrassing at 30 years old) to buy a cheap car and I found a sales job, that I hated, but it paid the bills. Karen was able to secure a job in the food industry and the money machine clicked into action.

A few years later we found ourselves with plenty of money for the big house, nice new cars (including a sports car for me), new furniture, clothes and a few fun trips. Life became about making more money to improve our lifestyle, under the guise of providing a good life for our children (over time, Karen's children all came to live with us).

Our lives experienced a shift in 1991 when our oldest daughter, who was 15 at the time, hooked up with a "bad boy". After several months, we told her she couldn't date him anymore. She ran away from home and began living at his house, with his mom. He told her that we were beating our daughter (which wasn't true) and they needed to protect her. For a time, we didn't know where she was or if she was okay. We later discovered that he was dealing and using drugs and had gotten our daughter involved in drug use, as well.

Things turned around when I received a call from our daughter who was in the hospital. He had beaten her, and she was not in good health. I went to the hospital and told her that we loved her, and she could come home.

She ended it with the boyfriend and began going to a church youth group with a friend. We watched her life dramatically turn around. She was visibly different. It was attractive, first to Karen, who also began going to church with our other children. I was still a hold out – hanging on to that promise I made, twenty years prior, when I was 18, but the Hound of Heaven was hot on my heels and He had a plan.

Discussion for Chapter 1: Beginning

1. What is your church back ground, if any, and how did it impact your life?

2. Were there any dramatic events in your life that ended up drawing you to God?

3. Did you ever have a moment when you considered ending your life? If so, what stopped you?

4. What impacted you most from the first chapter and why?

CHAPTER TWO

†

FOLLOWING

After Jesus was baptized by John, received the Holy
Spirit, and was led by the Spirit into the desert for
forty days of testing, he was walking along the
seashore one day and saw two Jewish brothers, Simon
(Peter) and Andrew. They were fishermen, probably in a
long line of professional fishermen. They were not born
into the right class, so they weren't disciples of a Jewish
Rabbi. They were uneducated men. Likely, they had heard
rumors about this guy, Jesus. After all, he had stood up in
the Synagogue and declared that he was the fulfillment of
Isaiah's Messianic prophecy:

> *"The Spirit of the Lord is on me, because he has
> anointed me to proclaim good news to the poor.
> He has sent me to proclaim freedom for the
> prisoners and recovery of sight for the blind, to
> set the oppressed free, to proclaim the year of the
> Lord's favor."* Luke 4:18-19]

Simon and Andrew probably looked at Jesus and

thought he looked like an ordinary guy, but there was something magnetic about him. Then he walked up to them and said, *"Follow Me and I will make you fishers of men."* [Matthew 4:19 NKJV] Here's the amazing part, they immediately dropped their nets and gave up their fishing business to follow him.

Later Jesus did the same thing to James and John, who were also fishermen. In fact, it says they left their father and fishing business to follow Jesus. This was probably a generational fishing business.

Next, we have Matthew, the tax collector. Jesus walked up to him and said, "follow me" and Matthew immediately stood and followed Jesus. When Matthew walked away from his tax collecting business to follow Jesus, he was giving up his profession and income source. Although much hated by the Jews, tax collecting was a very lucrative profession. We see another example of this in Zacchaeus, another hated tax collector, who after meeting Jesus agreed to give half his goods to the poor and restore four-fold to anyone he had cheated (Luke 19:1-10).

Follow You?

What amazes me most is that none of them seemed to ask any questions. Think about it. If Jesus walked into your office and said, "Follow Me", what would you do? If you are like me, you'd probably ask where are we going? How long will we be gone? What are we going to do? How will we make money? We might even be like the two other disciples (Matthew 8:18-22) who said they wanted to follow Jesus, but either had excuses or weren't willing to pay the price (of giving up their own way). Perhaps we might even tell Jesus to give us a couple months to bank some money, so it would be easier when we follow him.

Simon (Peter), Andrew, James, John, and Matthew could have all given Jesus excuses. Give us an hour or so to hang up these wet nets and get the boat secured; or let us go talk with our father about this whole idea of following you; or I'll need a couple hours to find a replacement for my tax collection booth. Oddly they didn't. They immediately got up and followed Jesus. That's what a true disciple does.

I'd like to say that when I first heard Jesus say "follow me" I immediately jumped up and followed him, but as I said previously, I was holding firmly to a promise made when I was 18, to never set foot in another church.

At the point when I went to the hospital to get our oldest daughter, I was around 38 years old, so it had been 20 years since that promise was made. Through those years, I met several Christians who invited me to church or Christian business events, but I still wasn't ready.

God's Timing

It took another two years for me to get ready. After the experience with the abusive boyfriend, drugs, and the hospital visit, our daughter became a regular at church. It was amazing to watch her life change. She was much less stressed, performed better in school, and was happier. Karen and the kids would head to church every Sunday. I just waved goodbye and enjoyed my time of solitude, reading the Sunday paper and watching sports.

God was starting to get my attention, as I could see Karen and the kids changing, but I was still angry and empty. I had tried to fill that empty place with alcohol, sex, money, worldly love, family and recognition, but nothing seemed to fill the void.

My family would arrive home from church so happy and talking about what an amazing time they had. They often referenced the incredible worship time. I knew it had to do with music, but my only reference was the one organ-accompanied hymn we sang every Sunday at the Presbyterian church.

Although I don't have a musical bone in my body, music has always moved me and so in the end it was music that God used to draw me in. By this time my family was attending services twice on Sunday and Wednesday night. One Sunday morning, I told Karen I might join them for the service that night. She told me later that she did a little happy dance in the walk-in closet.

I walked into the huge foyer of the Assembly of God church that night and was greeted by a friendly older man. I was hoping they wouldn't recognize me as an outsider and either kick me out or smother me. After all, my last experience with church people was not a good one. However, from the foyer into the sanctuary, people left me alone. I was also secretly hoping that God wouldn't zap me with lightning or something, because of all the bad stuff I had done.

Back then, my image of God was as an angry ruler who watched for me to do something wrong and then zapped me with some bad circumstance (I'm glad that I've learned that God is a loving and kind Father, who wants the best for His children).

After about 45 minutes of worship I was hooked, and God finally had me where He wanted me. It was as if the music were connecting with my very soul. Jesus was calling out, "Follow Me".

True disciples are not just church attenders; they are followers and students of Jesus. They want to go wherever Jesus goes and to do whatever Jesus does. They aren't content with a once a week service, they want to be friends with God, as Moses was.

"The LORD would speak to Moses face to face, as one speaks to a friend. Then Moses would return to the camp, but his young aide Joshua son of Nun did not leave the tent." [Exodus 33:11]

True disciples want God to speak with them face to face, as one speaks to a friend. Through Jesus, we have access to the throne room of heaven, and we can go confidently and boldly before the Lord any time we want (Hebrews 4:16), so why wouldn't we want to take advantage of that privilege?

God is our Father and He loves us. He wants the best for our lives. True disciples will set aside time every day to sit with the Creator of the Universe to receive His love and directions for the day.

Jesus often went away to a quiet place and spent time with the Father in prayer. The Bible says that sometimes he spent all night in prayer. A true disciple and follower of Jesus will do what he did. If you want to be a true disciple, I recommend time in the Gospels and the book of Acts to see what Jesus did and then follow his examples.

Discussion for Chapter 2: Following

1. Put yourself in the shoes of Simon, Andrew, James, John and Matthew. Would you have followed Jesus? Why or why not?

2. What is your "follow me" story?

3. The disciples gave up everything to follow Jesus. What excuses are you using to not fully follow Jesus?

4. What is the Holy Spirit telling you to do, that you haven't done?

CHAPTER THREE

†

SAVED

In my childhood, I spent many hours at swimming pools taking lessons and although I achieved a proficiency at the strokes, I was never very comfortable in the water. I could never figure out why, but I seemed to have a fear of the water. I later learned that it wasn't a fear of the water, it was a fear of drowning.

That almost happened in my Junior High days. I am part of the Baby Boom generation (those born between 1946 and 1964) that overwhelmed the school system and so in my first few years of Junior High, we were in the High School building. The Senior High attended in the morning and we were there in the afternoon, but there was a bit of overlap in the middle. Unfortunately, that overlap included my gym class. One day we were in the pool and had to tread water for 15 minutes. I had my back to the diving board and was already struggling, when one of the High Schoolers jumped off the board into me. I went under the water and started to panic. Fortunately, the Life Guard was quick to act and pulled me out. He saved me, and I was grateful.

In this world, there are many people, like the Life Guard, who save us from physical death. There is only one person who can save us from spiritual death. His name is Jesus and it's important to understand why we need to be saved by him. So, now let's go back to the real beginning; back to Genesis chapters 1, 2, and 3.

In these beginning chapters of the Bible we see the three-person God (Father, Son, and Holy Spirit) creating the universe and the earth. They then filled the earth with trees, plants, rivers, lakes, oceans, mountains, animals of every kind, and finally humans – male and female, created in God's image. These are perfect people, living in a perfect world, communing with God every day and living the life.

Oversee Paradise

God told the man, Adam, that his job was to oversee the paradise known as the Garden of Eden. Although there were many trees in the garden, God talked with Adam about just two of them. The first was the tree of life, the fruit from which would enable Adam to live forever. The second, was the tree of the knowledge of good and evil, from which Adam was never to eat or he would die.

To make a long story shorter, Adam and Eve were deceived by the serpent (Lucifer, now known as satan or the devil) into eating from the tree of good and evil, and both sin and death (physical and spiritual) entered the world. Adam and Eve did not immediately die physically, but their physical bodies began the death process. Their spirits immediately died and lost connection with God.

God is holy, and holiness cannot be in the presence of sin, so out of love for His children, He had to banish Adam and Eve from the garden. Mercifully, they were no longer allowed to eat from the tree of life, or they would have spent all of eternity dealing with guilt, shame and separation from God (likely some of the aspects of hell).

Contrary to what most people believe, God has emotions and shows them quite often throughout the Bible. I'm sure that He was grieved on that day, when He had to send His children out into the hard, cruel world that was now tainted by sin. He had created these god-like beings for relationship and now He could no longer draw close to them.

In the glories of heaven, the Godhead devised a plan for redemption. The Son would leave heaven to be born of a woman, by the Holy Spirit and be named Jesus; which means God saves or God is salvation.

Because Jesus was born of a woman and the Holy Spirit, he did not have the sin nature that had been passed on through the man since the fall of Adam and Eve. This was important, because Jesus needed to live a sinless life so he could become the perfect sacrificial lamb for all mankind.

Jesus lived a relatively normal life until he was around thirty and then God told him it was time to get to his life mission – to save mankind from its sin. If you don't already know, the penalty for sin is death – not physical death, rather spiritual death.

It's Your Choice

Those who choose to die in their sin are sentenced to hell, which is a place God created for Lucifer and the angels that followed him in rebellion against God. It was never created for man, only for those who rebel against God. Those who rebel against God, by not accepting Jesus as Savior, will make the choice to spend eternity in hell.

When Jesus died on the cross, he offered a "Get Out of Hell Free" card to every person on earth. All they had to do was receive the gift of salvation. In other words, just as I was drowning in the swimming pool and the Life Guard saved me, everyone is drowning in their sin and in need of a Savior. Jesus is the only one who can save. By just believing that he was the Son of God, born of a virgin, lived a sinless life, took the punishment for all sin (past, present, and future), was resurrected by the Holy Spirit, donned a new heavenly human body, appeared to hundreds of people for 40 days, and now sits at the right of the Father in heaven, we can be saved. That's it. We don't have to work for our salvation, it's a gift. Just believe in your heart that Jesus is your Savior, confess it with your mouth, and you are saved.

That Calvary Moment

I want to take a moment to reflect on what happened that day over 2,000 years ago in Calvary. I think so often we just pass over what an amazing thing Jesus did. Because of the sin nature we are born with, we have all sinned. Romans 3:23 says, *"for all have sinned and fall short of the glory of God"* and Romans 6:23 says, *"For the wages of sin is death, but the gift of God is eternal life in Christ Jesus our Lord."* Again, this is referring to spiritual death and the penalty, eternity in hell.

I digress a bit to discuss hell, because again, I don't think we talk enough about hell in our church services. It's not very politically correct, but to understand why we need Jesus as our Savior, we must understand what's going to happen to us, if we don't receive his gift of salvation.

As I mentioned earlier, hell wasn't created for man, rather for Lucifer and the third of the angels who rebelled against God. However, anyone who rebels against God by sinning, and who doesn't repent and receive Jesus as Savior, will also be sent to hell.

Through Jesus, God gives everyone a way out, so when people ask me why a loving God would send people to hell, I always say, "He doesn't, we do". We make that choice to receive the gift of salvation or not.

Those who don't accept salvation and die in their sin will find themselves in a place more horrifying than anything imaginable. Jesus talked about hell several times and made sure that people knew that he didn't want them there. He wanted them in heaven, which is why he willingly gave up the glories of heaven, set aside His God attributes, to be born a helpless baby and then die a horrific death on a cross.

Hell is a Real Place

Hell is referred to as the *"fiery lake of burning sulfur"* (Revelation 21:8). If you've ever read about hot sulfur, it burns hotter than any other type of fire, plus the smell is awful. It's also referred to as a *"blazing furnace, where there will be weeping and gnashing of teeth"* (Matthew 13:50). My take on this is that the pain will be so horrific that people will grind their teeth and scream.

Jude 1:7 describes hell as a place of *"eternal fire"*, so it's not like you get burned and then have time to get better, it's constant burning for all eternity (that's a long time of suffering).

Mark 9:48 says about hell, *"where the worm does not die, and the fire is not quenched."* We don't hear much about people getting eaten by worms, but from what I've read and heard, it is a most painful death and in hell people will have the pain, but no relief of death.

Finally, 2 Thessalonians 1:9 tells us that in hell people will experience *"everlasting destruction"* and will be *"shut out from the presence of the Lord and from the glory of His might."*

That's the one that really got me. Even if a person doesn't believe in God, he or she is still experiencing God's presence on the earth. Again, even if we don't recognize it, we feel His love and light, because that is who He is. Imagine, for a moment, the horrible feeling of not having

God's love and light present. Hell, is a place of total darkness, completely shut off from God, where people with eternal bodies that don't die, are tormented with fire and worms for all eternity and with no hope of it ever changing!

It boggles my mind that anyone would ever make the choice to go to hell. It's even more mind boggling when I hear people say that they would rather go to hell, than heaven, because all the fun people will be in hell. Well, it's not true that all the fun people will be in hell, and those who are there certainly will not be having any fun.

Back to My True Disciple Story

Okay, thanks for allowing me to take you on an important rabbit trail, now back to the cross. I'm grateful to my spiritual mentor, Tim Johnson, who taught me the truth about the cross and what Jesus had to endure for me (and you).

First, was the mental agony of having so many people calling for his death and then all his close friends abandoning him.

Second, he was beaten to the point of extreme pain, but no broken bones.

Third, they jammed a crown of one-inch thorns into his head.

Fourth, they whipped him with a cat of nine tails. This is a handle with multiple bits of glass, metal, or bone tied at the end of leather straps. The Romans were masters of torture and excelled at wrapping the straps around the body and ripping down to the bone. With 39 lashes, they could whip someone to the point of death, but keep them alive. This is what they did to Jesus.

Fifth, after the severe beating, they forced Jesus to carry a heavy wood beam, on his torn back, through the streets, with people on all sides jeering and spitting at him. He fell so often, that they finally forced a man named Simon (not

Simon Peter or Simon the zealot) to help carry the cross.

Sixth, they took huge metal spikes and drove them through the palms of his hands and into the beam. Then they crossed his feet and drove a larger spike through the tops of both his feet.

Secure on the cross, several soldiers picked up the cross and dropped it in a hole, jarring Jesus' body on the cross and causing even more excruciating pain. People who are crucified don't die from loss of blood, they die from shock and asphyxiation; they get to a point where they can't push themselves up to take a breath and so they die an extremely painful death.

The Father Turns Away

As if that wasn't bad enough, before Jesus died, the Father, who had spent eternity past with the Son in loving community, placed all the sin of mankind on Jesus. Think about how you feel with just a little bit of sin. Imagine experiencing all the horrific sin in the world – child molestation, violent rape, mass murder, hate, envy, lust, gossip, and so much more – all at one time. Plus, for the first time in eternity, the Father turned away from the Son. This is why Jesus said, *"My God, my God, why have you forsaken me?"* (Matthew 27:46)

Jesus took all the sin, all the pain and agony, all the punishment that we deserved and then announced, *"It is finished!"* (John 19:30). The legal transaction that covered and paid the price for all sin in the past, present, and future was complete. Physical death still existed, but spiritual death and eternity in hell was defeated on the cross. From that point on, all people had to do was follow instructions:

> *"If you declare with your mouth, 'Jesus is Lord,' and believe in your heart that God raised him from the dead, you will be saved."* Romans 10:9]

That's it. It's that simple! Believe in Jesus, confess it with your mouth and you get to walk with God the rest of your life and enjoy the glories of heaven (no pain, no sickness, no sorrow, no death) for eternity!

Now, I'm going to jump up on a soapbox for a moment, because I think we've gotten fixated on the salvation prayer too much in the modern church. It's not about the prayer, it's about believing in Jesus and what he did on the cross and then confessing that belief out loud.

You can be saved in your bedroom, bathroom, kitchen, backyard, classroom, work place, in an airplane, hotel room, cruise ship, spaceship, or anywhere else you can think of. You don't have to say any particular prayer, all you have to do is admit that you are sinful and headed to hell and accept Jesus as your one and only Savior, and you are saved.

Jesus already took your penalty, so you can be confident in your walk with God here on earth and your eternal life in heaven, once you pass on from this world. There is nothing you can do to lose your salvation.

I Must Continue

Sorry, I must continue on my soapbox a little longer. It's interesting that Jesus never led the disciples in a salvation prayer. Peter didn't lead the 3,000 in a prayer of salvation on the day of Pentecost.

There is no record of Philip the Evangelist ever leading someone to the Lord with a prayer. Even the Apostle Paul, who wrote much of the New Testament didn't use a salvation prayer to get people saved. They just believed and were saved. Ok, I'm finished.

My moment of salvation occurred a few months after attending that first service at the Assembly of God church. It happened at a dramatic event called Heaven's Gates and Hell's Flames. This was a traveling theatrical troupe, who brought sets and props, and used local church members to perform an evangelistic drama program.

The night I attended there were over 2,000 people in the audience. Part of the set included steps leading to heaven and a podium with the Book of Life. In vignette after vignette, normal people died of heart attacks, car accidents, or were murdered.

After death, they would face Jesus, who would look in the "Book of Life" (Revelation 20:15) and if he found their name, they would climb the stairs into heaven. Those who had accepted Jesus as their Savior were those who had their names written in the Book of Life. If Jesus did not find their name, then he would shake his head and loud demonic music would begin playing, red and white lights flashed, and ugly demons would drag the person screaming into hell (this is not biblical, but it was very compelling).

I'm Going to Hell!

I was horrified to watch this scene played out over and over and recognized that, because I had not yet accepted Jesus as my Savior, I was going to hell. I tell people that this performance scared the "hell" out of me and when the pastor called for those who wanted to accept Jesus, I couldn't get down to the altar fast enough. In fact, I was sitting in the balcony and was afraid I might trip down the stairs, fall, die, and end up spending eternity in hell. At that time, I didn't understand that I didn't have to get to the altar; that my belief in Jesus and confessing him as my Savior, would save me.

That night I was "saved", but over time I've realized that salvation is not a one-time experience. I was saved, am being saved, and one day, when Jesus returns as the conquering King, I will be completely saved. Salvation is a process. Now, please don't misunderstand me. We aren't saved by doing good works, but rather by our faith in Jesus as Savior. The moment I realized I was going to hell and accepted Jesus as my Savior, I was saved. From that point on, as the Apostle Paul said in Philippians 2:12, I am *"working out my salvation with fear and trembling"*.

When we have that moment of spiritual clarity and are saved, our spirit is revived, and we are filled with the Holy Spirit. Once again, we are in right relationship with God and can feel confident in the presence of the Lord, as Adam and Eve did, before the fall. That said, our soul (mind, will, and emotions) and our body (flesh) still need some saving.

You can be saved, filled with the Holy Spirit, attend church weekly, read your Bible daily, and still sin. The sin is covered by Jesus' death, but it does impact how we feel about our relationship with God and can keep us from growing close to Him. Thus, the need to work out our salvation with fear and trembling.

Beyond following Jesus, the first step toward true discipleship is salvation. To be a true disciple of Jesus, you must be saved. If you are not saved and are feeling that tug at your heart, it's time to confess your sins to God and profess Jesus as your Savior and you will be saved. That's just the beginning of your salvation experience.

Discussion for Chapter 3: Saved

1. If you aren't saved, now is the time to repent of your sins and receive Jesus as your Savior. If you are saved, briefly share your salvation story with the group.

2. The author described what Jesus endured, out of love for you. Describe how that makes you feel.

3. Salvation is a gift, but that's just the beginning. What are you doing to walk out your salvation with fear and trembling?

4. Have you ever had a moment when you thought you might not be saved? Briefly share that with the group.

CHAPTER FOUR

†

BAPTIZED

When I was a wee child (that's my Scottish ancestry coming out), I was sprinkled at the Presbyterian Church, which they referred to as baptism. After my salvation experience, I began reading the Bible and was surprised that, for the first time in my life, I could understand what I was reading.

Well, it might have helped that I had an NIV Life Application Bible (which my kids gave me for Father's Day), rather than my old fake leather zippered KJV Bible, but I also had the Holy Spirit living in me. Reading through the gospels I noticed something interesting. It seemed like baptism was something different than sprinkling a baby.

In the four gospels of Matthew, Mark, Luke, and John we see John the Baptist dunking people in rivers and calling it baptism. In fact, he baptized Jesus in the river. I began to study baptism and saw that all throughout the New Testament, people would get saved and then immediately baptized by full immersion in water. It became clear to me that baptism was not part of the salvation experience, but rather an outward demonstration of salvation.

Our church offered regular baptisms, so several months after I was saved, Karen and I signed up to be baptized. We first had to attend a class, where they checked to make sure we were saved and then explained the significance of baptism and the reason it required full body immersion. The water represents the grave. Going under the water represents death and burial. Raising back out of the water (I was thankful that I didn't need a Life Guard this time) represents resurrection to new life.

> "I have been crucified with Christ and I no longer live, but Christ lives in me. The life I now live in the body, I live by faith in the Son of God, who loved me and gave himself for me."
> [Galatians 2:20]

Fortunately, we did not have to be literally crucified on the cross with Jesus. He did it for us and took all the shame, pain, and agony. We get all the benefits, without the pain. Being baptized, through full water immersion, is the outward expression of Galatians 2:20 and confirmation that someone is truly saved.

One of my favorite stories in the Bible is Philip and the eunuch:

> "Now an angel of the Lord said to Philip, 'Go south to the road—the desert road—that goes down from Jerusalem to Gaza.' So he started out, and on his way he met an Ethiopian eunuch, an important official in charge of all the treasury of the Kandake (which means queen of the Ethiopians). This man had gone to Jerusalem to worship, and on his way home was sitting in his chariot reading the Book of Isaiah the prophet. The Spirit told Philip, 'Go to that chariot and stay near it.' Then Philip ran up to the chariot and

heard the man reading Isaiah the prophet. 'Do you understand what you are reading?' Philip asked. 'How can I,' he said, 'unless someone explains it to me?' So, he invited Philip to come up and sit with him. This is the passage of Scripture the eunuch was reading: 'He was led like a sheep to the slaughter, and as a lamb before its shearer is silent, so he did not open his mouth. In his humiliation he was deprived of justice. Who can speak of his descendants? For his life was taken from the earth.' The eunuch asked Philip, 'Tell me, please, who is the prophet talking about, himself or someone else?' Then Philip began with that very passage of Scripture and told him the good news about Jesus. As they traveled along the road, they came to some water and the eunuch said, 'Look, here is water. What can stand in the way of my being baptized?' 'If you believe with all your heart, you may.' The eunuch answered, 'I believe that Jesus Christ is the Son of God.' And he gave orders to stop the chariot. Then both Philip and the eunuch went down into the water and Philip baptized him. When they came up out of the water, the Spirit of the Lord suddenly took Philip away, and the eunuch did not see him again, but went on his way rejoicing. Philip, however, appeared at Azotus and traveled about, preaching the gospel in all the towns until he reached Caesarea." [Acts 8:26-40]

There are many things I love about this scripture account. First, I love that God sent an angel to direct Philip to a divine intersection with the Ethiopian eunuch. Second, that Philip was in good enough shape to run alongside the moving carriage and still talk. I have trouble walking on the treadmill and talking. Third, I love that Philip was able to bring clarity to the scripture the eunuch was reading. Finally, when Jesus said "follow me" to the eunuch's spirit, he did, and immediately wanted to be baptized.

Another great baptism story can be found in Acts 16:32-34. Let's set the stage. Paul and Silas are in prison and not like any prison we've seen. This is a dungeon, their hands and feet likely bound in stocks, sitting in pools of refuse and excrement, and surrounded by rats.

So, it's about midnight and Paul and Silas are praying and worshipping God (not griping and complaining like most of us would), when suddenly there is an earthquake and not only do all the prison doors open, but the stocks fall off. All the prisoners are free, but none of them leave – that's the power of the presence of God.

An Earthquake

The jailer is awakened by the earthquake and can see that all the doors are open. He draws his sword to kill himself, when Paul cries out that they are all still there. He falls trembling under the presence of the Lord and says, *"Sirs, what must I do to be saved?"*

Paul and Silas replied, *"Believe in the Lord Jesus, and you will be saved - you and your household."* The jailer then took Paul and Silas to his house (remember that this is after midnight), cleaned them up, and then he and his whole household were all baptized. It says that they were so filled with joy because they had come to believe.

True disciples are not only followers of Jesus, they are saved and baptized. If you are saved and have not been baptized through full emersion, check with your church or find someone, who believes in Jesus and has been baptized, who will baptize you in a local pool, lake, or river.

Discussion for Chapter 4: Baptized

1. Why are we to be water baptized?

2. If you have been baptized, briefly share that experience with your group.

3. In Galatians 2:20, what does, "I have been crucified with Christ" mean to you and in your life?

4. Paul and Silas were worshipping in prison. What circumstances do you have going on in your life, in which you should be worshipping, rather than complaining?

CHAPTER FIVE

✝

TRANSFORMING

Let's go back again to after the moment I confessed Jesus as my Savior. Although I was saved at Heaven's Gates and Hell's Flames, I wasn't seeing much life change. I was still struggling with the same thoughts and was still angry. Several people said that I needed to renew my mind with the Word of God, the Bible.

> *"Do not conform to the pattern of this world, but be transformed by the renewing of your mind. Then you will be able to test and approve what God's will is—his good, pleasing and perfect will."* [Romans 12:2]

At that time, I only had a zippered, fake leather-bound King James Bible that my Grandmother gave me when I was nine and had never been able to read it. The only Word I had coming into my mind was what I heard at the one service per week, which is like eating one small meal once a week and expecting to be healthy. Fortunately, as I mentioned earlier, my kids gave me an NIV Life

Application Study Bible that next Father's Day and the Word came alive for me and I began my transformation.

Further transformation occurred when I joined a group of guys from the church at a Promise Keepers event in the Seattle Kingdome. I had several life changing experiences there. The first occurred when we arrived, and I had to use the restroom. When I emerged, my group was gone. I thought they were going to wait for me and we didn't have cell phones back then, so I had no way to contact them.

I wandered the main concourse inside the dome for a few minutes and was marveling at all the men (over 60,000). Suddenly, I heard a booming voice say, "ROD". I said, "Yes, Lord?" Then I realized it was just one of the younger guys who had been with a different group on the bus. He invited me to sit with them.

Amazing Grace, How Sweet the Sound

Another powerful experience was when 60,000 men sang Amazing Grace. Normally, I don't think of a bunch of men sounding heavenly, but it was a beautiful, heavenly sound. It was at that PK event that I had my true heart salvation and came back a different person. Karen often talks about how different I was, when I came home that night. God finally had my heart!

On the bus ride home, some of the guys and I were talking about starting some men's small groups, as that had been a primary message at the conference. It was at that moment that God set my heart on fire for men's ministry and I've been active in it ever since.

Upon arriving home, I set an appointment with the associate pastor who oversaw men's ministry. In our meeting, I excitedly told him I'd like to join or start a men's small group and help with men's ministry. He informed me that they didn't have a men's ministry or any small groups. I was shocked. This was a church with over

2,000 attending every weekend and they had a women's ministry that met every Wednesday with about 200 women attending. I told him that I didn't know anything about starting a men's ministry, but I was a quick learner. He said that they had unsuccessfully tried to start men's ministries in the past. I asked if he had any issue with me starting a men's small group. He was fine with that.

A week later twenty-one men from the PK conference started meeting weekly to go through the PK book, *Brothers*[1], which taught us how to start small groups. From those twenty-one guys we launched four small groups that eventually became the nucleus of a very vibrant men's ministry, that I was blessed to oversee for five years.

God Wanted a Men's Ministry

I guess God wanted a men's ministry at the church, because that associate pastor ended up moving to another state to take over as the senior pastor of a church and a younger Associate took over who was excited about having a men's ministry.

Apparently, God had missed so many years with me (I was 40 at this point), that he wanted me on a fast track of learning. I had never read the Bible (mainly because all I had ever seen was the King James and I couldn't read it – still can't), yet with my new NIV Life Application Bible in hand, God began to teach me His Word. I was amazed at how much of it I understood – more than anyone around me expected.

Ordinary Men

The same was said of Peter and John. After they received the Holy Spirit on the Day of Pentecost, they began preaching Jesus boldly, which drew attention from the religious leaders, and they were placed in jail. The next day they were standing in front of the rulers, elders, teachers of the law and the high priest. Peter, filled with the power and boldness of the Holy Spirit, begins preaching the gospel of Jesus. It says in Acts 4:13:

> *"When they saw the courage of Peter and John and realized that they were unschooled, ordinary men, they were astonished and they took note that these men had been with Jesus."*

The religious leaders recognized that Peter and John were unschooled and ordinary men. They were not born into a family where they studied under a Rabbi as children. They were just ordinary men. In fact, we know that they were both fishermen prior to following Jesus. What made them different was that they had been with Jesus.

To be a true disciple, we too need to spend time with Jesus. Since we can't do that physically, we must invest time every day studying and meditating in the Word of God. The Word will wash away the old carnal thinking and replace it with spiritual thinking, so that we are not as apt to conform to the ways of the world. This is particularly important as we head toward the end of time here on earth.

Matthew 24, a chapter that talks about the end times, gives us a warning about being deceived in verse 24:

> *"For false messiahs and false prophets will appear and perform great signs and wonders to deceive, if possible, even the elect."*

We are already seeing false teachers and prophets who are teaching and prophesying things that draw people away from Jesus and further down the road to hell. If we don't invest time in the Bible, we might be among the "elect" who are deceived and though I don't believe we could lose our salvation, we certainly could be misled and confuse others who aren't saved. The answer is to invest time daily in the Word of God – study, meditate, and memorize scripture to protect ourselves from cunning deception.

There are many countries where it's illegal to have a Bible, go to church, and even be a professing Christian. Here in the United States we have religious freedom, but that freedom is shrinking fast and it's very possible that we may encounter a time where Christians in the United States are persecuted, churches are closed or destroyed, and Bibles are scarce. It will be important that we have the scriptures memorized and planted in our heart of hearts.

Beyond that, the only way we can transform our soul (mind, will, emotions) and body (flesh) is through the Word of God. If you struggle with anger, the Bible can help you conquer that. Can't seem to escape sexual lust? The Word of God can give you the strength to battle your way out. Are you a liar, gossip, thief, slanderer, cheater? Transforming your mind with the scriptures is the answer.

Stay Pure in this Crazy World

How can we stay pure in this polluted world? Psalm 119:9 (NLT) says that it's by obeying God's Word. Having the Word inside you and allowing yourself to be guided by it and the Holy Spirit, will enable you to make decisions based on God's will and not your own. I found this out the hard way.

In my first year of salvation, we were doing quite well financially and one day, I bought a brand-new T-top Camaro. It was a beautiful metallic green, and frankly, I loved that car. I remember at times walking away and looking back to admire it. The problem was that I didn't pray and ask God about this purchase. I didn't even talk with Karen beforehand. It was completely a carnal decision.

Even then, with just a little bit of Word in me, I had a

sense that I shouldn't have bought it. Well, one night at a men's Bible study, God told me I had made the car an idol. I immediately rebuked the devil (ha-ha). In all seriousness, I knew that it was God speaking. He continued to speak with me about this idol, but I didn't do anything, so He took care of it for me.

On a cold January night, we experienced a one-of-a-kind ice storm. In the over 30 years I lived in Tacoma, WA, it was the only time it ever happened. I had the Camaro parked under our carport and you can probably guess what happened.

Yes, the ice was so heavy that the carport collapsed, and the main beam and all the ice crushed the T-top. The car was in bad shape. The difficult part for me was that it was so new that we weren't sure if the insurance company would pay to fix it. In the end they did, but everyone told me that the T-top would always leak. We got the car back, good as new, with no leaks and immediately traded it in on a lesser car.

The Rest of the Story

Here's where the story gets interesting. We had never liked the carport, but didn't want to pay to have it torn down and hauled away. Our homeowner's insurance paid us $6,000 for the carport and covered having someone do the clean-up. The exciting part was that our oldest daughter was getting married in a few months and that was the exact balance we had on the wedding costs.

> "*And we know that in all things God works for the good of those who love him, who have been called according to his purpose.*" [Romans 8:28]

If you liked that car story, here's another one. We traded the Camaro in on a barely-used Honda Civic. It was red and a little sporty – big rims and a sun roof. We had the car for two days and it was stolen during the night. Karen and I immediately prayed that it would not be involved in any kind of illicit activity and that we would get it back. The police told us that there was a 2% possibility we would ever see the car again, and if we did, it would be in bad shape. Two days later, they called and said that the car had been found and it was actually in fairly good condition. The thieves had stolen the tires, wheels, stereo, bucket seats, much of the plastic in the dash, center console, and the airbags.

There were a couple things we didn't like about the car. First, were the big rims and small tires, as they made the car ride hard and noisy. Second, was the 6 CD changer, as at that time, in 1996, we had a huge collection of cassettes and only a few CD's.

God Turns it to Good!

The insurance company paid for new tires and wheels, of our choosing, and a new stereo system with speakers. We picked out a great combo deck with CD and Cassette player and Bose speakers. Plus, we ended up with new bucket seats, a new dash and console. The car looked new inside and there was no outside damage. What the enemy meant for evil, God turned into something good.

Talk about faith building and seeing that God can turn any bad situation into something good. God did a lot of that early in my walk with Him. Again, I think He was making up for lost time.

The Bible is our instruction manual for life. Everything you need to know about how to live life is in there – you just have to choose to read and study the book. Joshua 1:8 (NLT) says:

"Study this Book of Instruction continually.

Meditate on it day and night so you will be sure to obey everything written in it. Only then will you prosper and succeed in all you do."

Now, this doesn't mean you have to become a monk in some mountain monastery, quit sleeping and just study scripture every moment of every day. Rather it means to go beyond reading your daily quota of scripture and really think about what you are reading. Study it. Ask God to reveal things for your life. Memorize scriptures, so you have them in your heart. That way you can meditate on them when you are driving or in the shower or even while you are sleeping (yes, the subconscious mind can continue meditating on scripture).

It was during these early days that I fell in love with the Word of God. I began to read and study voraciously, devouring scripture like a hungry man. Again, this made sense, since I had 40 years without the Word, so I was spiritually starving. Jesus called himself the "bread of life" and we also know that he is "the Word" from John 1.

When I was reading the Bible, I was consuming the bread of life and that's exactly what it did, it gave me new life and it will do the same for all the true disciples.

GIGO

There is nothing that will transform the mind quicker than meditating in the scriptures. There was an old computer term GIGO (Good In, Good Out), which described that the good information entered would produce good output. Since our minds are like computers, what we put into them, will determine what comes out. If we fill our minds with the bad news, smutty novels, pornography, racy movies, and negative secular talk radio or TV, what comes out isn't going to be good. Rather, if we put the Word of God into our minds every day, good will come out.

Since my salvation, I have spent thirty minutes to two hours each morning reading and meditating in the Word. I've read through the Bible at least eight times from front to back (which I highly recommend, as it provides a much better understanding of the whole story). There have been times when God had me in a single book of the Bible for a month or more. Because I now fill my mind with scripture and live it daily, negative emotions such as lust, anger, jealousy, envy, selfishness, and accompanying sinful actions do not come out very often. Instead, more often than not, the fruit of the spirit (Galatians 5:22) will come out. I'm still a work in progress and will be until Jesus takes me home, but I'm a much better man now than I was before I started studying the Bible and became a doer of the Word (James 1:22).

The Mysterious Class Catalog

Another transforming experience occurred about three years after I was saved. I had just finished a men's ministry committee meeting and was sitting in the sanctuary waiting for my family to arrive for service. I had been thinking about taking one of the classes the church offered, so I picked up the catalog of classes. When I opened it, all I could see was one class. Everything else seemed to be blurred out. I even went back and looked at another catalog to see if the one I had was a misprint. It wasn't, as again, I could only see one class.

God clearly wanted me to attend that class. However, when I read the description, it sounded very advanced, beyond where I was, but because it was the only class I could see in the catalog I decided to go.

Nervously, I walked in the door and quickly scanned the group, thinking I could still back out. Sure enough, these were all the leaders in the church and I was just turning to leave, when I heard someone shout my name. Bounding across the room was one of the young men who had been in the original men's group of 21. He hugged me and said that he had been praying I would come to this class. I was hooked!

The class was called Discipleship Training School and was taught by a non-staff pastor, Tim Johnson. Unquestionably, this class rocked my world. It was an intense study with two hours per week in the classroom, homework from the class, two books to read, and a book report to complete in twelve weeks. Every week I arrived home and, out of excitement for what I had learned, would preach the message to Karen. I finally understood the complete Bible story, how the Old and New Testaments fit together, what a blood covenant was, why Jesus had to die on the cross, and the impact his death and resurrection had on us. Most importantly, I finally knew that God wasn't mad at me; in fact, He loved me.

A Table Leader

Upon completion of the class, Tim asked me if I would consider being a table leader for the next session. I said yes, and also asked him if he would consider mentoring me, which he agreed to do.

At the time, Tim and his Dad owned a construction company about an hour south of me. Weekly I would make the long trek to have lunch with Tim and pick his spiritual brain. We became very close and later planted a church together. We remain close today and I will be forever grateful to him for all he poured into me.

Tim asked all the table leaders to attend a spiritual retreat that he was leading. They kept talking about how strong the Spirit was at these retreats and how they would pray for two or more hours. Since I had never really prayed, I kept wondering what you could possibly pray about that would take two hours.

At that retreat, we had three and a half hours of wonderful prayer time with the Lord. This was the first of many mind-blowing retreats, that Karen and I attended with this group of amazing people.

During one of the retreats, I experienced my first sense of "timeless" heaven. We know that there is no time in God's realm, as He operates outside of time. At this particular retreat, we began praying at 3:00 in the afternoon and we "awakened" from prayer at 10:00 pm. This was a camping retreat, so we found ourselves in the dark, unaware of where everything was. I guess we could have used some of Jesus' light at the time, but finally flashlights and lanterns were found.

Soaking in His Presence

We enjoyed long times of prayer (three to seven hours) at every retreat and it was during those times that I learned to press into God and soak in His presence. I transferred this practice into my quiet times at home and have received many revelations during those times. Our lives are so busy and noisy; sometimes it's hard to hear God. He loves it when we take a break from the busyness, find a quiet place, and invest time with Him.

No Agenda

One caution though, don't go into these times with an agenda or list. Go in to listen. At first it will feel odd, but if you remain quiet, you will begin hearing God's still small voice through your spirit. It probably won't be an audible voice, rather a thought that lines up with the Word and is applicable to something you are praying about.

For the disciples that walked with Jesus, transformation didn't occur instantly, it took time and it's the same for us. It's also not a one-time deal. We are always transforming to look more like Jesus. Devote time studying the Word of God, join a small group Bible study to discuss scripture with other believers, attend services with the body of Christ to hear great teaching, and set aside quiet time to spend with the Lord to listen and pray. God will use all of these to transform you into a True Disciple.

END NOTE

1. https://www.promisekeepers.org.nz/product/brothers

Discussion for Chapter 5: Transforming

1. Why is renewing your mind important?

2. When did God finally get your whole heart? If not, what's holding you back?

3. Discuss your current Bible study activity and ways you could improve that.

4. Talk about any classes you could take and why you haven't before now.

CHAPTER SIX

✝

FAITH

In this chapter I'm going to share what I've learned about faith and how important it is to the true disciple, but first I want to share a story about faith in action. At 3:00 am on Thanksgiving in 2005, I was awakened by the Lord, so that He could share with me a new ministry plan. He laid out plans for Karen and I to launch 4 the Lord Ministries - a traveling teaching ministry. We were to be Messengers of Hope to a struggling nation.

Over the next four hours and eight pages of legal-size paper, God revealed the details of this amazing ministry. When He was done talking and I completed the notes, He said something that shook me to the core, "Go". That was it, just "Go". I asked Him where we were going and again, He said "Go". I asked when we were to go and again, He said, "Go". After that, every question was met with mind blowing silence.

I began to question whether I had really heard Him, but "Go" kept rising up in my spirit. I remembered how God had told Abram to go and did not tell him where he was going, so I felt that was confirmation.

A couple weeks later, Karen was in prayer and she received a date, January 10th and had a vision which gave us confirmation that our ministry would be on the West Coast from north border to south border. Later, we received two prophetic words, from people we trusted. The first was just the word *Southwest* and the second was that we had *an open door in Temecula*. We weren't sure what either of those meant, so we continued in prayer and heard nothing more from the Lord. On January 10th, 2006, we loaded up the car and began driving. We lived in Tacoma, WA, which was about as West as you can go, so we headed South on Interstate 5.

Off Ramps

As we drove, we spent hours worshipping God and praying. At times we would sense the Lord wanted us to take an off ramp. On one occasion, we found a man in a store who needed prayer. On another we met a single Mom and her young son who were stranded. We were able to pray with them and help them with the funds they needed for car repairs.

Off another exit, we were led to a church, but the enemy caused suspicion in the person we met inside the church and so we were unable to do whatever the Lord intended. We attempted to set a time to meet with the pastor, but again God's plan was thwarted by the enemy, so we shook the dust off our shoes and continued the journey.

After a couple days, we still weren't sure where we were going, but God was starting to share more about our ministry. We were also to be ministers of hope to pastors, which seemed very strange, until we met with our first pastor and he started gushing with all the struggles in his life. It was clearly a Holy Spirit inspired time and we were able to pray for him, the church, and bring hope back into his life. We encountered other pastors who were on a fast track to quitting the ministry and the Holy Spirit breathed new life back into them through our words of hope.

As we drove, we continued to ponder the prophetic words of Southwest and the open door in Temecula. We had been in communication with a family member living in Southern California. She was struggling as a single parent and was feeling hopeless. We sensed that this was to be part of our mission and God confirmed it, so we continued to head south with her home as our initial destination.

Prophecy Fulfilled

We arrived at about 7:00 pm on Saturday and talked with her until 1:00 am. In the morning, she wanted to take us to her church, so we all dressed and piled into her van. As we entered the church, she introduced us to several people, including the pastor, and then we settled into our seats to await the start of service. I looked at the bulletin and realized that we were at Southwest Christian Church in Temecula, CA. Tears filled my eyes, as I recognized the fulfillment of both prophetic words in one place. The church and pastor were truly an open door for us, as he encouraged us and our ministry.

We invited the pastor to lunch to see if other doors might open. After the server took our order, the pastor said to her, "In a moment we're going to pray for our food, is there anything we can pray about for you?" She told him several things about her life and when he prayed for our meal, those were included in the prayer.

Karen and I were so struck by the power of this, that we began praying for the server every time we were at a restaurant. We were amazed at the personal things they were willing to share, and we included in our prayer, as we blessed our meal. Many times, we were able to deliver messages of hope to them before we left.

One of the Sundays we were in southern California, we

visited a small church that met in a school. The pastor and his wife greeted us at the door, and we told them a little about us, our background and ministry. After the service, the pastor invited us to lunch, and as with the other pastors we had encountered, shared his woes in ministry. We were able to share some words of hope with him. One of his struggles was regarding both personal and church finances, so I gave him a copy of my book, *God's Prosperity Plan*, and suggested he read it and implement what he learned. He agreed to do exactly that. He said that our words had been invaluable and timely. God had put us in the right place, at the right time.

I had booked a speaking engagement at a large business event in San Diego for the following Tuesday. We were at that event, when the pastor I had given the book to, called and said that he read the book and wanted to know if I would speak on Sunday.

A Powerful Prophetic Word

That Sunday I delivered a word on God's plan to prosper His children and during the message issue a prophetic word for the church. Their church services had been held in a high school for many years. They had owned a large piece of land, but the funds weren't available to build a building. I told them that God was giving them wisdom to get that building built within the next two years. After the message, many people blessed us with financial gifts that kept us on the road.

We returned to that same area, in southern California, a couple years later to discover that God brought a real estate expert into that church. He helped them sub-divide the land, sell a piece of the property, and then use the funds to build a beautiful church building. God is so good!

As suddenly as God had said "Go", He told us to return to our home in Tacoma. We continued ministering hope to congregations and pastors all the way up Interstate 5 and throughout Washington state for two years. It took a lot of faith to just "Go", but God abundantly blessed us and many others on that trip. I'm so glad that Karen and I both had learned about faith and how to walk in it; otherwise, we would have missed out on an amazing, life-changing experience.

I remember early in my walk with the Lord, my mentor, Tim Johnson, taught us about faith. He pointed to a church chair and said, "You can believe that this chair is solid and will hold your weight, but it's not faith until you sit on it." For the first time I recognized that there is a difference between belief and faith. Let's examine those differences, beginning with belief.

Dictionary.com defines belief as "confidence in the truth or existence of something not immediately susceptible to rigorous proof."[1]

Merriam-Webster defines belief as "Conviction of the truth of some statement or the reality of some being or phenomenon when based on examination of evidence."[2]

Vine's Dictionary defines belief as "to place confidence in, to trust, reliance upon."[3]

Belief relates to how you think about something, but faith requires an action on that belief. You can believe that your clock will wake you at the right time, but only if you have set it for the correct time and the sound is on high enough for you to hear the alarm. You can believe that you will excel at your job, but only if you do more than what the job requires and come in every day with a great attitude. You can believe that your spouse and kids will always love you, but only if you are unselfish in your love for them. You can believe that Jesus will save you, but only . . .

When it relates to Jesus, many people believe in him as a historical figure, a prophet, a good man, a teacher, a rabbi. Even satan and his fallen angels (demons) believe in Jesus. This may sound a bit radical, but belief in Jesus will not save you. For about thirty years, I believed in Jesus as a religious figure, but I was not saved. We can see that belief is not enough in Ephesians 2:8-9:

> *"For it is by grace you have been saved, through faith—and this is not from yourselves, it is the gift of God—not by works, so that no one can boast."*

Grace is the gift offered by God to every person through the sacrificial death of Jesus, but it must be received through faith and by just believing or by works. This is where it gets a bit dicey, so let's do a quick study of faith.

Dictionary.com defines faith as "obligation of loyalty to a person, promise, engagement; or the observance of this obligation."[4]

Merriam-Webster defines faith as "strong belief or trust in someone or something."[5]

Vines Dictionary defines faith as "firm persuasion; a conviction based upon hearing."[6]

If we go into the Greek, we find that the word that is translated as faith is *pistis*, which is defined as "conviction of the truth of anything; belief with the predominate idea of trust; fidelity and faithfulness."

I believe the best definition of faith can be found in Hebrews 11:1:

> *"Now faith is the confidence in what we hope for and the assurance about what we do not see."*

Faith is like the power that comes into your home. All your lights, appliances, computers, and televisions are plugged into electrical outlets and have power, but none of them work unless you switch them on. We have confidence or belief that the power is there (if we've paid our electric bill). We can't see the power, but there is assurance that it will be there when we need it.

Faith allows us to access the power of God. Just like electricity, we can't see the power. Jesus already paid the price with his death and we have the assurance through the Holy Spirit and the Word of God.

As we study belief and faith, we see that they are interrelated, but not the same. Belief is a lower level of commitment than faith. As we saw in the chair example earlier, belief is thinking that the chair will hold you, but faith is the action of walking over and putting that belief to the test by sitting in the chair.

I've experienced the difference between belief and faith when it comes to healing. For a long time, I was afraid to boldly ask someone if I could pray for their healing, so I would just pray for them from a distance. I never saw any healings. It was when I would feel the tug of the Holy Spirit to lay hands on someone and pray, that I would see results. I still struggle with this at times.

Recently, I was in a fast food restaurant waiting to order and the girl in front of me mentioned that she was deaf in one ear. I felt that prompting of the Holy Spirit, but didn't do anything.

I know that if I had been able to lay my hand on her ear and pray for healing in the powerful name of Jesus, she would have been healed. I did pray for her quietly and believed she would be healed, but she didn't suddenly start hearing. The faith action of speaking with her and laying a hand on her ear was missing. Ah, we live and learn.

Another area where I've seen a clear distinction between

belief and faith is in the financial area. I can believe that God will provide the money we need to live, but if I don't move out in faith by first seeking the way He wants me to earn an income (a job, business, or ministry), then tithing and giving, nothing will happen. Contrary to some popular prosperity teachings, we can't just sit at home and watch TV or play video games and expect God to bless us. 2 Thessalonians 3:10 says that if we won't work, we won't eat. God expects us to work and then He can bless us with money. If we tithe and give, He can bless us with more. When we step out to work, tithe, and give, we are operating in faith and that gives God something to work with.

I often think of faith as building materials for God's plan in our lives. If you were a contractor, building a house would require materials – concrete, wood, nails, siding, windows, etc. God also needs building materials to build our lives. The Apostle Paul talks about this in 1 Corinthians 3:10-13:

> *"By the grace God has given me, I laid a foundation as a wise builder, and someone else is building on it. But each one should build with care. For no one can lay any foundation other than the one already laid, which is Jesus Christ. If anyone builds on this foundation using gold, silver, costly stones, wood, hay or straw, their work will be shown for what it is, because the Day will bring it to light. It will be revealed with fire, and the fire will test the quality of each person's work."*

In this scripture, we see that only Jesus can lay a solid foundation for our lives and then God uses our faith actions as building materials. If we try to build under our own strength, we build with inferior materials that will burn up in the revelation fire. We need to step out in faith and let

God use that faith to build solid lives.

So, how do we build our faith? Romans 10:17 says:

"Consequently, faith comes from hearing the message, and the message is heard through the word about Christ."

We can believe that God exists, and Jesus died on a cross for our sins over 2,000 years ago, but faith comes when we hear the Word of God from an apostle, pastor, teacher, prophet, or evangelist or by read the living Word of God and hearing that message with the Holy Spirit confirming it. Then we step out in faith to profess Jesus as our Savior and allow Him to be Lord over our lives.

True Confessions of an Agnostic

I remember for many years debating with people over the validity of the Bible. I would say that it was just a bunch of stories and myths, written by men and probably, knowing how men are, greatly exaggerated. Plus, I would talk about how over the thousands of years of translation, the Bible probably didn't even say what it originally did.

I was very good at debating and definitely swayed a few people away from the Bible and Christianity, for which I've repented, as their names came to mind. The truth was that I had never even read the Bible.

In my BC (before Christ) days, I believed in Jesus and had heard all the stories about him being born in a manger on Christmas day, but I didn't know that I needed him as my Savior. That didn't come until I heard the message, through the Word of Christ. I had belief, but faith was required for me to understand and receive God's grace to be saved.

Faith is for more than salvation. It's a form of heavenly currency. It enables us to see into the Kingdom of God and to pull things from heaven onto earth. That's why Jesus taught his true disciples to pray:

> *"Your Kingdom come, Your will be done, on earth as it is in heaven."* [Matthew 6:10]

He was teaching the disciples to use their faith to bring God's Kingdom to earth, so that earth could become more like heaven.

After Peter professed Jesus as Messiah, Jesus told him:

> *"And I tell you that you are Peter, and on this rock, I will build my church, and the gates of Hades will not overcome it. I will give you the keys of the kingdom of heaven; whatever you bind on earth will be bound in heaven, and whatever you loose on earth will be loosed in heaven."*
> [Matthew 16:18-19]

Jesus was telling them that the key to accessing the Kingdom of heaven (or God) is to use their faith to bind (forbid) the activities of satan and his demon army, so that they would be bound in heaven and could not work. He also told them to loose (approve) into the earth, things that are in heaven – divine health (vs. sickness), prosperity (vs. poverty), joy (vs. sadness and depression), love (vs. hate and violence), peace (vs. stress) and more.

Heaven is perfect and we know that the earth is not. Jesus gave his true disciples the authority (more on this in chapter 8) to make earth more like heaven by healing people with diseases and physical ailments, raising the dead, delivering people from demonic possession and oppression, preaching the Kingdom of God with power, and receiving the finances necessary to fund personal needs and ministry work. This authority was (and still is) accessed and implemented through faith.

Jesus told the disciples that with faith as small as a mustard seed (the smallest seed), they could move mountains, and nothing would be impossible for them (Matthew 17:20). Peter proved this when he did the impossible and walked on water, but as he began to doubt and fear, Jesus had to save him and responded:

"You of little faith, why did you doubt?"
[Matthew 14:31]

Wow! With little faith, Peter walked on water. With little faith, the disciples healed and raised people from the dead. With little faith, we are saved and assured of eternity in heaven. Imagine what we could do with big faith!

So, belief is the starting point of faith. We must first believe and then we can put our faith to work in that area. If we are sick, we must first believe that God heals and then we can speak to the sickness in faith and command it to leave. Now, there may be another step of faith necessary and that's going to the Doctor or Hospital. God also uses Doctors in the healing process.

Financial Struggles

If we are struggling financially, we must believe that God doesn't want us poor and begin speaking to our finances in faith. We do this by speaking financial scriptures as declarations over our finances. Now, again, there is another step in that we need to have a way to make money – job, business, or ministry. God isn't going to rain money down on you or materialize a sack of money in your living room or a money tree in the backyard. Perhaps it will be different for you, but I've asked many times and it hasn't happened, yet. We also need to be good stewards of what God gives us.

Faith is a partnership between us and God. As we hear

and read the Word of God, we begin to believe, and we can put our faith to work; then it's up to God and He is always faithful. That said, He doesn't always respond in the way we want or in our timing. In fact, in my experience, He rarely responds the way we want or in our timing. God's ways and timing are bigger and better than ours, so part of the faith process, is to leave all that up to Him and rest (mentally and spiritually, but not physically).

The end of Hebrews 3 and into 4 talks about God's rest. To enter God's rest, we must completely surrender to Him and we can only do that by faith. The first-generation Israelites missed out on His rest when they left Egypt and lacked the faith to enter the promised land.

The second-generation Israelites entered the promised land, but also did not have the faith to enter God's rest. It's still available to us, as long as it's still today (until Jesus returns and heaven comes to earth). We can enter that rest through faith.

Jesus described this rest in Matthew 11:30:

"For my yoke is easy and my burden is light."

In the world the yoke is hard and harsh, and the burden is difficult and stressful. The Israelites experienced the hard yoke and burden as slaves in Egypt and then the easy yoke and light burden, as God provided everything they needed.

When we are resting (in God's rest), we aren't using any of our own power (although we are still doing things), we are relying solely on God's power (His will, not ours be done). Our world is hard and stressful, but we can still enter God's rest by faith, and He will provide what we need.

As we close out this chapter, it's important to know that according to Hebrews 11:6, *"without faith it is impossible to please God"*. True disciples want to please God. We first do that through salvation and then by living by faith and not by sight (2 Corinthians 5:7). We are spiritual beings living in fleshly earth suits. The world trains us to live by sight and to only believe what we can see. Well, the unseen world is more real than what we can see. The unseen or supernatural world was here before this chunk of rock we call earth, was created by God. The unseen world is more powerful than the world we see. To please God, we must be able to access our faith and see into the unseen world. Jesus said he only did what he saw the Father do and as true disciples, we should be operating the same way.

As true disciples, we should be accessing our measure of faith (Romans 12:3) to study and meditate in the Bible and pray every day. We should use our faith to conquer any habitual sin activities. Faith can help us be more selfless in our marriage and to love like 1 Corinthians 13:4-8 teaches. We can access our faith to be good parents, workers, business owners, money managers, and servants in the church body and community. Faith is the answer to living the abundant life referenced in John 10:10.

Access More of Your Faith

As we access more of our measure of faith, we can speak healing into people's bodies (by the name of Jesus), we can speak to weather, we can rebuke demon voices and bind their activities, we can cast demons out of the possessed and away from the oppressed, we can operate in God's protection, power, favor, and blessing. We can go into the world and share the good news about Jesus and salvation. We can make disciples who make disciples. We can feed the hungry, clothe the naked, house the homeless, give hope to the hopeless, visit the prisoners, and take care of the widows and orphans. The people who have been financially blessed can help those who are struggling, as if they were the hand of God (which they are). Churches and ministries can be launched and funded through faith.

In three different places (Romans 1:17, Galatians 3:11,

and Hebrews 10:38) the Bible teaches us that *"the righteous will live by faith"*. We, who are saved, are the righteous (in right relationship with God). As I mentioned earlier, 2 Corinthians 5:7 says that we are to *"live by faith, not by sight"*. In other words, we are to live by listening to the Holy Spirit, who will guide us and we should not pay too much attention to our natural senses.

We do need senses to operate in this natural world, but when it comes to the things of God, He is working through the Holy Spirit to open our spiritual eyes to see what He's doing and our spiritual ears to hear His still small voice.

In the world, it's easy to rely on our natural senses and enter into fear - when we see the huge bill and know that there isn't enough money in the bank account; when the doctor says its stage 4 terminal cancer; when the boss says they are downsizing, and you are out of a job in a bad job market. Fear is the opposite of faith. Fear is the devil's language and faith is God's language. Fear will kill you and faith will result in life abundant.

Fear is a lie and faith is truth. Think of fear this way:

F = False
E = Expectations
A = Appearing
R = Real

False expectations appearing real. So, you are getting ready to go into a job interview and your mind begins playing all the bad things that are going to happen. Are any of those real? No, they are false expectations that appear real to the mind. Scientific studies[7] have proven that the mind can't tell the difference between reality and a firmly placed visualization. Premier athletes have used this for years, as they visualize ski runs, golf and basketball shots, winning the big game, knocking out the opponent to win the title, hitting a grand slam to win the World Series, making the buzzer beater shot to win the NBA championship. All these things have happened, but when the person was visualizing them, they weren't real at that moment.

The only power satan/the devil has over us is through our thoughts. He can float fearful thoughts toward us and if we accept them, he can continue to water those seeds with more powerful fear thoughts. This only works if we accept them. However, we can recognize that those fearful thoughts are not from God and reject them. It's for this reason that the Apostle Paul taught the church in Corinth to *"take captive every thought to make it obedient to Christ"* (2 Corinthians 10:5).

Reject Those Thoughts

We aren't to just receive every thought that comes into our mind, as if it were from God. Those thoughts could be from our carnal mind, from the demonic realm, or from God. We are to compare every thought to Christ, the Word. In other words, our thoughts should line up with the Bible. If they don't, then we are to reject them.

By the way, fearful thoughts (unless we are in a life-threatening situation) are always from the demonic realm, so reject them and use faith to think about the promises of God.

Now, I hear some of you thinking, but what about the fear of God? That's a totally different type of fear. It's a faith fear. In other words, it's faith in an awe inspiring, almighty God. *"Fear of the Lord is the beginning of wisdom"* (Psalm 111:10) and *"Fear of the Lord is the beginning of knowledge"* (Proverbs 1:7).

God is certainly to be feared. If it were not for the blood of Jesus covering our sin, we would be subject to the same wrath as those we see in the Old Testament. God is Holy and as such cannot tolerate sin. In fact, a Holy God who did not deal with sin would not be a God worthy of our worship. However, God doesn't want us to fear Him, as we might an attacking lion or a person with a gun. Rather, He wants us to respect Him and His ways.

It is through faith that we show our reverential love and respect for God and just by operating with a little of our measure of faith, we can please God. The true disciples always want to please God, so get into the Word of God and learn how to access more and more of your measure of faith and you can change the world!

END NOTES

1. www.dictionary.com
2. www.merriam-webster.com
3. Vines Dictionary Android App
4. www.dictionary.com
5. www.merriam-webster.com
6. Vines Dictionary Android App
7. David R. Hamilton, PhD, "Does Your Brain Distinguish Real from Imaginary?", Using Science to Inspire, accessed 8-23-16, http://drdavidhamilton.com/does-your-brain-distinguish-real-from-imaginary

Discussion for Chapter 6: Faith

1. Have you ever felt God telling you to do something? Briefly describe what happened.

2. Share with your group if you have ever received a prophetic word and what happened.

3. Briefly share what faith means in your life.

4. What do you need greater faith for in your life? Have the group pray with you.

CHAPTER SEVEN

†

PRAYER

P rayer is interesting to me. Although I grew up in church, I never remember praying except on Sundays at services. We didn't pray before meals or before bedtime. So, when I got saved and everyone talked about prayer, I didn't know what to do. As I mentioned earlier, after taking the Discipleship Training School class, I was asked to be a table leader and go on a spiritual retreat. They said we would pray for two hours or more and I remember thinking what in the world could you pray about for two hours? It was during those retreats that I learned how to pray.

I find it very interesting that Jesus, the Son of God, often went off by himself to pray, sometimes all night. Yet, most Christians don't pray five minutes per day. Why? I think there are three reasons. First, life is busy and so people devote time to things that are urgent or fun. To most people, prayer isn't either urgent (except in a dire situation) or fun. Second, there aren't a lot of sermons on prayer and so people don't understand the importance of it. Third, most people don't know how to pray and so they don't.

Jesus's disciples were no different than those in the church today.

> *"One day Jesus was praying in a certain place. When he finished, one of his disciples said to him, 'Lord, teach us to pray, just as John taught his disciples.'"* [Luke 11:1]

The disciples could see that Jesus prayed, but they didn't know how, so they asked. The Bible says we have not, because we ask not (James 4:2). How many things are you wondering about, but aren't asking for answers?

In answer to his disciples asking him to teach them about prayer, Jesus responded in Matthew 6:9-13:

> *"This, then, is how you should pray: 'Our Father in heaven, hallowed be your name, your kingdom come, your will be done, on earth as it is in heaven. Give us today our daily bread. And forgive us our debts, as we also have forgiven our debtors. And lead us not into temptation, but deliver us from the evil one.'"*

Luke reported Jesus' instructions in Luke 11:2-4:

> *"He said to them, 'When you pray, say: Father, hallowed be your name, your kingdom come. Give us each day our daily bread. Forgive us our sins, for we also forgive everyone who sins against us. And lead us not into temptation.'"*

Now, let's clear something up right away. Jesus was not intending this to be a rote prayer repeated over and over, as some do. In fact, Jesus addressed this in Matthew 6:7, *"And when you are praying, do not use meaningless repetition as the Gentiles do, for they suppose that they will be heard for their many words."* Rather, Jesus intended this to be a model for prayer, so let's look at it in this way.

When you pray – Jesus didn't say, if you pray, he said, when you pray, so clearly, he intended for his true disciples to pray, as he did.

Our Father in heaven – This is a reminder of who we are praying to. We are not praying to Jesus or Mary or the Holy Spirit, we are praying to God the Father. Now, we do, as instructed by Jesus, pray in his name (John 14:13) and it is Jesus who will answer the prayer. Jesus was first teaching respect and awe for the Father in heaven.

It's a reminder that we are talking with our heavenly Father, who loved us so much that He sent His only Son to die for us, so we could be in right relationship with Him. We don't have to be formal with Him – no old English needed – just talk with Him like you would your earthly father or any other earthly father figure. You are His child and He loves hearing from you.

Hallowed be Your name – This means to honor God's name. His name is holy. In fact, there have been times when people would not even speak or write the names of God, out of reverential fear. Don't come to prayer with God flippantly, rather come with the respect God deserves. There is a fine line between talking with Him as a Father, and not showing Him respect by being too casual. I've heard people refer to God as dude and the big guy upstairs; that's too casual.

Your Kingdom come – When Jesus died on the cross, God restored authority over the earth to mankind and established the first part of the Kingdom on earth. It will not be complete, until Jesus comes as the conquering King and rules on earth.

At that time the cursed earth will be restored and will be like Eden was in the beginning. The new Jerusalem will come down out of heaven and it will literally be heaven on earth for all eternity. That's the future Kingdom come.

In the meantime, those of us who are saved/born-again, can operate in the Kingdom through the Holy Spirit living in us. It is our responsibility to advance the Kingdom throughout the earth, by sharing the good news of salvation and by making disciples.

Your will be done on earth as it is in heaven – In heaven there is no sin, no evil, no sickness, no pain, no sorrow, no tears, no death, everything is perfect. It was God's will that the earth be the same as heaven, but sin and darkness has infected everything. That said, Jesus showed us that as believers we can bring bits of heaven to earth through our prayers.

Give us this day our daily bread – This is a reference to when God supplied daily manna for the Israelites in the desert. Each morning they would awaken to find a layer of manna on the ground. They were to gather exactly what they needed for the day and no more, except on the day before the Sabbath when they were to collect enough for two days. Any manna they tried to save would spoil. The next day there would be more. God was showing them that they could trust Him to provide day by day. He's saying the same thing now. God is our provider, not our job or business or retirement account or investments. All of those come from God and can be easily taken away or destroyed. However, when we rely on God as our provider, we will never lack. Matthew 6:33 says:

"But seek first his kingdom and his righteousness, and all these things will be given to you as well."

And forgive us our sins, for we also forgive everyone who is indebted to us – This is saying that because God forgave our sins, we also forgive those who offend or sin against us. Matthew 6:15 teaches:

"But if you do not forgive others their sins, your Father will not forgive your sins."

Jesus told a story about a man who owed millions and asked for forgiveness. His creditor forgave the debt, but the man immediately went out and demanded a small debt be repaid. The original creditor found out and threw the forgiven man in prison (Matthew 18:21-35).

God has forgiven us a great debt and He expects us to forgive others. In Matthew 18:21-22, Peter asked Jesus:

"'Lord, how many times shall I forgive my brother or sister who sins against me? Up to seven times?' Jesus replied: 'I do not say to you, up to seven times, but up to seventy times seven.'"

Jesus was telling Peter that God never stops forgiving and so he shouldn't either and neither should we.

And do not lead us into temptation, but deliver us from the evil one – I have always interpreted this to mean, do not allow us to be tempted, because James 1:13 teaches that God doesn't tempt us. That said, God will allow us to be tempted by things of the world and by satan. Jesus was led into the wilderness by the Holy Spirit, to be tempted by satan.

Another example is Job. God had placed a hedge of protection around Job (Job 1:10) and satan could not tempt him. Our prayers can do the same thing. That doesn't mean that nothing bad will ever happen, because there are still many evil people in the world, and they all have a free will that God will not go against. But, it's a good thing to pray every day, because our flesh and mind can certainly follow temptation and get us into a lot of trouble.

To reinforce, this is a prayer that Jesus gave to his disciples as a model. You do not need to pray it word for word every day. You can if you want, but don't let that be your only prayer. Talk with God all day - in the shower, eating breakfast (in between bites, please – God doesn't like "seefood"), driving to work, throughout your workday, driving home from work, before you eat a meal (remember what Jesus did for you on the cross), before you go to sleep, and any other time it comes to mind. You don't have to close your eyes (particularly if you're driving). It's a conversation with your heavenly Father.

It's a Conversation

That brings up a great point – it's a conversation. If you have a conversation with your spouse or a friend where all you do is tell him/her what you want and then walk away, how would they feel about you? God isn't Santa Clause or some magical genie. So, don't just come to Him with your list of needs and wants. He does want to hear those, but He also wants to hear about your day – the bad and the good. He wants to know what you are learning in scripture. He wants you to ask questions and He will answer. He probably won't answer in an audible voice, rather through the still small voice in your spirit, through scripture, teaching, or conversation with another person. When you meet with God, don't do all the talking; leave quiet times for Him to talk.

Jesus spent a lot of time praying. I believe that when he spoke with the Father, he was given his upcoming assignments. In fact, in John 5:19, Jesus said:

"Very truly I tell you, the Son can do nothing by

himself; he can do only what he sees his Father doing, because whatever the Father does the Son also does."

Jesus never did anything on His own. He also never said anything that he didn't first hear the Father say (John 12:49). I don't know about you, but I think that if Jesus needed to get with the Father regularly to find out what to do and say, we need to even more. That's what prayer is all about.

There are two types of prayer that the Apostle Paul mentions in 1 Corinthians 14:15:

"So what shall I do? I will pray with my spirit, but I will also pray with my understanding; I will sing with my spirit, but I will also sing with my understanding."

So far in this book, prayer refers to the second type, *"pray with my understanding"*. In other words, praying in your native earthly language, in my case, that would be English (and probably yours, unless you're reading a translation of this book). But, Paul mentions a second type of prayer and that's what we're going to examine next.

Paul said, *"I will pray in the spirit"*, but what does that mean? I can't say that 100% of the Bible scholars would agree, but most believe that Paul is talking about speaking in tongues, which he references as a spiritual gift in 1 Corinthians 12:10, *"Still another person is given the ability to speak in unknown languages..."* Then he references tongues very heavily in 1 Corinthians 14 (we will cover this in detail a little later). Jesus also said that speaking in tongues would be one of the signs that accompanies those who believe in him (Mark 16:17).

I received my spiritual tongue at one of our retreats, around three years after I was saved and baptized. I was skeptical of tongues, even after hearing it regularly and my wife receiving her language. It wasn't until my spiritual mentor, Tim Johnson, gave an inspired and complete teaching on tongues at a retreat. All my concerns melted away and I was ready to receive. I asked and the Holy Spirit released my gift. I've been speaking in tongues ever since and it's amazing!

Tongues is a gift, given by the Holy Spirit. Although not all Christians speak in tongues, it is available to everyone who has the indwelling of the Holy Spirit (which happens at salvation). Tongues can be utilized in two ways, first as a prayer language in your private time with God, and second, as a sign to unbelievers that God is present (1 Corinthians 14:22).

We see the latter in evidence on the Day of Pentecost, when the Holy Spirit arrived to indwell the true disciples (Acts 2). All 120 in the room received the Holy Spirit and spoke in tongues. The unbelievers who were attracted by the sound of the Holy Spirit, came and heard them speaking in their native languages.

I believe, that if we study the actual language in Acts 2, we discover that the disciples where not speaking in those languages, rather they were speaking in their heavenly language (as enabled by the Holy Spirit) and the Spirit was allowing the unbelievers to hear in their own language.

Let's look at Acts 2:8 to confirm:

> *"Aren't all these who are speaking Galileans? Then how is it that each of us <u>hears</u> them in our native language?"* (emphasis mine)

I believe that if the disciples were actually speaking the native languages, it would have said, Aren't all these who are speaking Galileans? How is it that they <u>speak</u> in our native language?

Now, just because you speak in tongues in public,

doesn't mean that other people will hear it in English or any other language. Make sure you are strongly directed by the Holy Spirit, before speaking in tongues publicly. Also, as we see in 1 Corinthians 14, tongues can disturb church gatherings, so unless your pastor or a church leader invites people to speak in tongues, knowing that there is someone present with the gift of interpretation (1 Corinthians 12:10), don't speak in tongues loudly in a gathering. You can speak quietly, during a worship time and during prayer times, but keep in mind what Paul said in 1 Corinthians 14:4, *"Anyone who speaks in a tongue edifies themselves..."* Tongues is for building up yourself, not the body of Christ.

Utter Mysteries

That said, if we go back to 1 Corinthians 14:15, we should pray in the spirit, which is in tongues, during our private time with God. In 1 Corinthians 14:2, Paul says that *"For anyone who speaks in a tongue does not speak to people, but to God. Indeed, no one understands them; they utter mysteries by the Spirit."*

A couple keys in the scripture we just read, first when we speak in tongues we are speaking directly to God. I believe that tongues is a language only God can understand. The devil can't understand our prayer and react.

Second, we are speaking mysteries directly from the Holy Spirit, who is in us, to Father God. That means we are praying the perfect prayer; exactly what is necessary at that time. Paul reinforces this in Romans 8:26:

> *"In the same way, the Spirit helps us in our weakness. We do not know what we ought to pray for, but the Spirit himself intercedes for us through wordless groans."*

So, if you have a time when you don't know what to

pray, pray in tongues and the Spirit will pray the perfect prayer. It may sound like groans or gibberish, but it's perfect!

Perhaps you are wondering how to begin speaking in tongues? Ask the Holy Spirit to release the gift and then speak. Don't get concerned about what it sounds like, as it will sound strange. Any time you hear someone speaking in another language it sounds different.

Don't Listen to the Lies

Also, don't let the devil convince you that it's not real. If you have asked the Holy Spirit for your prayer language and something that doesn't sound like your native language comes out, then you are speaking in a heavenly language. It may start as just a few syllables. The more you use your language, the more it will grow.

Don't be concerned if you don't speak right away. Ask God to reveal any unbelief or lies that are hindering the activation of your spiritual tongue. Finally, once you receive your tongue, don't worry that you will be out of control and start speaking in tongues when you don't want to. God is a God of order, not disorder. You will always have control over when you speak and when you don't.

Ready for Your Spiritual Language?

Don't have your spiritual language? Get into a quiet room and invite the Holy Spirit to help you release your language. When you feel something kind of bubbling up, open your mouth and speak. Relax and let it go. As it flows, you will feel an excitement in your spirit, because you are speaking directly to God in a heavenly language. Just like you have a different DNA from anyone else in the world, I believe you also have a different language than anyone else. Oh, it may sound similar to someone else, but they are all unique. It's your private language to use with God. Wow!

A true disciple devotes time every day to conversation with God, in order to find out what to do and say, how to handle situations and people, make decisions of any kind, share needs and wants, and tell Him what you're excited about. A true disciple will also pray in tongues daily and throughout the day. Just like He did with Adam and Eve, God loves to meet and talk with His kids. He's just waiting on you.

Discussion for Chapter 7: Prayer

1. Discuss what prayer means to you.

2. Share a prayer story with the group.

3. Discuss ways you can improve your prayer life.

4. Have you activated your prayer language (tongues)? If not, have the group pray for it to be released.

CHAPTER EIGHT

†

AUTHORITY

Before we jump into authority, I want to establish the difference between power and authority. There are many out there who are operating in power – using the gifts given to them through the Holy Spirit, but they are not operating in authority. We can see this in the powerful ministers who have fallen. They were able to preach, lead people to the Lord, and disciple their followers by using their gifting (power), all the while struggling in hidden sin.

I can relate to this, as when God called me to be a pastor in 2001, I was still struggling off and on with pornography and anger (both of which God delivered me from later).

Dual Personality

When I speak about those years, I often say that it was like I was a dual personality. There was my spirit man who preached powerful, life changing sermons, taught classes, and wrote books. Then, there was my carnal man struggling in the darkness.

I continued operating in the power of the spiritual gifts I

received at salvation, but never operated in the authority of Jesus. It wasn't until later, when God completely delivered me from my many carnal issues, that I began to operate in both power and authority.

Jesus is a perfect example of a man who operated in both power and authority. It appears that for the first thirty years, he lived a pretty normal life. After his water baptism and receiving the Holy Spirit, Jesus began to operate in power and authority.

Wimpy, Wimpy, Wimpy

For most of the time the disciples walked with Jesus, they were kind of wimpy. They did and said stupid stuff (like we all do). They didn't operate in power and authority until after the baptism of the Holy Spirit on the day of Pentecost. It's that power and authority that changes the world.

I love the little book, *The Believer's Authority* by Kenneth E. Hagin[1]. It is the most powerful seventy pages you will ever read. In this book, Hagin defines authority as "delegated power". For example, an Army General has been delegated power by the U.S. government. While serving in the military, he has that authority. However, if he retires, he's still considered a General, but no longer has the authority. The good news is that as true disciples of Jesus, we have delegated power and authority from the Creator of the universe and we never retire.

Jesus operated in an authority that no one had ever seen before. We see this in Mark 1:22:

"The people were amazed at his teaching, because he taught them as one who had authority, not as the teachers of the law."

All the people were amazed, because Jesus seemed to be

a normal man and no other man had ever spoken with that type of authority or performed the miracles that he did. He exhibited authority over sickness, blindness, deafness, paralysis, disease, demons, storms, seas, plants, and even death.

Now, it would be easy for us to say that Jesus had that authority because He was the Son of God and that would be correct. He was the Word, who was there in the beginning and who created everything. John 1:1 says: *"In the beginning was the Word, and the Word was with God, and the Word was God."* Then in verse 14 it tells us that, *"The Word became flesh and made his dwelling among us."*

Jesus is the Word

The Word was Jesus, before He gave up the glories of heaven to be born as a baby, grow in wisdom and stature (Luke 2:52), be baptized by John the Baptist, receive the indwelling of the Holy Spirit, minister on earth for three years, and then die a horrific death to redeem all of mankind and bring us into right relationship with God. He then was resurrected, revealed himself in a glorified human body to over 500 people on earth, and then rose to his place at the right hand of the Father in heaven.

Fully God and Fully Man

Jesus was fully God, but also fully man. I know that's a bit mind boggling. I guess that's why in Isaiah 55:9, God says that His ways are higher than our ways and His thoughts are higher than our thoughts. This is one mystery we will likely never completely understand here on earth. However, Paul does give us a little insight into this.

In Philippians 2:5-8 (NASB), the Apostle Paul was teaching the Philippian believers that they needed to be more like Jesus:

"Have this attitude in yourselves which was also in Christ Jesus, who, although He existed in the form of God, did not regard equality with God a thing to be grasped, but emptied Himself, taking the form of a bond-servant, and being made in the likeness of men. Being found in appearance as a man, He humbled Himself by becoming obedient to the point of death, even death on a cross."

In the process, Paul is also teaching about Jesus, the man. Here it says that Jesus *was "in the form of God . . . but emptied himself."* Most theologians believe (and I agree) that Jesus emptied himself of his God attributes in order to be fully man. This makes sense, because Jesus couldn't be all powerful, all knowing, and everywhere at the same time, inside a tiny, helpless baby. He had to become fully man.

Jesus was the only sinless man, since Adam, so he likely operated in a greater fullness of the Spirit, but he was a flesh and blood man. He had to operate in life the same way we do. Jesus relied on communicating with the Father through the Holy Spirit inside. In fact, as we discussed earlier, Jesus himself said that he could do nothing by himself and he did nothing but what his Father was doing. He was operating with power delegated to him by the Father, through the Holy Spirit, whom Jesus received at his baptism.

Jesus also gave his disciples that same authority. Let's look at that in Matthew 10:1:

"Jesus called his twelve disciples to him and gave them authority to drive out impure spirits and to heal every disease and sickness."

In Matthew 10:8, Jesus also gave them authority to raise

the dead. Peter operated in that authority and raised Dorcas/Tabitha (Acts 9:40). Paul did the same when he raised Eutychus (Acts 20:9-12). There have also been many documented resurrections throughout church history. You can read about these in the book *Saints Who Raised the Dead: True Stories of 400 Resurrection Miracles* by Father Alfred J. Hebert[2].

Resurrection wasn't just for the former days, it's for today. Charisma News[3] reported that John Smith, a youth who spent 15 minutes at the bottom of an icy lake in Missouri and another 30 minutes with no pulse, was resurrected after a short prayer by his mother, and is now living a completely normal life. This resurrection story was turned into a movie, titled *Breakthrough* (2019).

Raising the Dead

In his book, *Raising the Dead: A Doctor Encounters the Miraculous*[4], Chauncey Crandall (a Palm Beach heart doctor) relates the story of Jeff Markin, a patient whose vital signs stopped as he lay in the emergency room. Declared dead at 8:05 on Sept. 20, 2006, Crandall sensed God telling him to pray for Markin, which he did quietly. After making one more attempt with the defibrillator, Markin's heart started beating. Although, he should have been a vegetable, Markin is now in his 60s and active in his church.

In the book and movie, *90 Minutes in Heaven*[5], we see Pastor Don Piper, who after a horrendous wreck, was declared dead by the EMTs. A minister arrived on the scene and prayed for Don, who miraculously returned to life.

Okay, if this seems kind of strange, that's okay. Resurrection is strange and uncommon in our society, but it wasn't strange to Jesus or the disciples/apostles or the many true disciples since that time. Any opportunity you get to pray for the dead, do so; particularly if they are not headed to heaven. What have you got to lose? They're already dead. The worst-case scenario is that they stay dead, but there is also the possibility that God just might send them back and WOW, what a testimony you would have!

Karen and I have discussed that if either one of us dies, the other is NOT to pray for resurrection. If I'm in the presence of my Savior, in the glories of heaven, I'm going to be really mad if someone prays me back. Now, if I die and God sends me back, because it wasn't my time, I'm okay with that.

Not Their Time

Now, I imagine that the only time people are prayed back to life is when it isn't their time and God sends them back. I think it's quite possible that there are times when someone dies, and they are given the option to stay or go back. If people are praying for them, they are more likely to choose to return to finish out their life on earth.

Let's move on to more about the authority of the believer. In Matthew 28:18-20, Jesus said:

> "All authority in heaven and on earth has been given to me. Therefore go and make disciples of all nations, baptizing them in the name of the Father and of the Son and of the Holy Spirit, and teaching them to obey everything I have commanded you. And surely, I am with you always, to the very end of the age."

In the way this is structured we can see that Jesus had the authority to make disciples and he was transferring that authority to his true disciples. This meant several things. They were given authority to heal, deliver people from demonic possession/oppression, raise the dead, and forgive sins. All this was done through the power of Jesus, not in their own power. No one can boast of healing someone or raising them from the dead, only the powerful name and authority of Jesus can do that. The good news is that we are in Christ and He is in us, so we have the same authority!

It's easy to see, from reading the New Testament, that Jesus had authority over physical body ailments, and he passed that authority on to all true disciples. Jesus healed the blind, deaf, mute, lame, and diseased. One of my favorite stories is when Jesus healed the leper in Matthew 8:1-3:

> *"When Jesus came down from the mountainside, large crowds followed him. A man with leprosy came and knelt before him and said, 'Lord, if you are willing, you can make me clean.' Jesus reached out his hand and touched the man. 'I am willing,' he said. 'Be clean!' Immediately he was cleansed of his leprosy."*

Since we don't deal with leprosy in the U.S., it's important to put this into perspective. First, it's a contagious disease that causes severe, disfiguring sores and nerve damage to the arms and legs. Because lepers were contagious (by touch) and often hideous looking, they were shunned and required to announce that they were in the area by saying, "unclean, unclean".

Second, any priest or rabbi who touched a leper would have been ceremonially unclean. So, for Jesus to talk with a leper was quite unusual and yet, his love was so great for this man that he touched him. Now, Jesus had healed people just by speaking, so he didn't have to touch the man. I've always felt this was an act of compassion, as the man probably hadn't been touched in years.

Again, it would be easy to say that Jesus healed because

ROD NICHOLS

he was the Son of God, but as I've already shown, that's not the case. Jesus was just an instrument of the Father's delegated authority. All believers, who operate in faith, have that same authority.

Let's go back to the Bible and look at a few examples of God healing people through the disciples. In Acts 3:1-10, we see Peter heal a lame man:

"One day Peter and John were going up to the temple at the time of prayer—at three in the afternoon. Now a man who was lame from birth was being carried to the temple gate called Beautiful, where he was put every day to beg from those going into the temple courts. When he saw Peter and John about to enter, he asked them for money. Peter looked straight at him, as did John. Then Peter said, 'Look at us!' So the man gave them his attention, expecting to get something from them. Then Peter said, 'Silver or gold I do not have, but what I do have I give you. In the name of Jesus Christ of Nazareth, walk.' Taking him by the right hand, he helped him up, and instantly the man's feet and ankles became strong. He jumped to his feet and began to walk. Then he went with them into the temple courts, walking and jumping, and praising God. When all the people saw him walking and praising God, they recognized him as the same man who used to sit begging at the temple gate called Beautiful, and they were filled with wonder and amazement at what had happened to him."

In Acts 9:33-35, Peter heals a paralyzed man:

"There he found a man named Aeneas, who was paralyzed and had been bedridden for eight years.

90

'Aeneas,' Peter said to him, 'Jesus Christ heals you. Get up and roll up your mat.' Immediately Aeneas got up. All those who lived in Lydda and Sharon saw him and turned to the Lord."

In Acts 5:15-16, we see that if Peter's shadow fell on someone they were healed. Now, that's power and authority!

In Acts 19:12, even handkerchiefs and aprons that had touched Paul were healing people.

Lastly, in James 5:13-15 it reads:

"Is anyone among you sick? Let them call the elders of the church to pray over them and anoint them with oil in the name of the Lord. And the prayer offered in faith will make the sick person well; the Lord will raise them up."

Once again, we see the connection between faith and authority.

Who are the elders referred to in the scripture we just read? They were the true disciples of Jesus. So, if you are a true disciple, you are a biblical elder. If someone says they are sick or you see someone in a wheelchair, walker, or on crutches, let them know that you are a follower of Jesus Christ. Continue by saying that sometimes when you pray, God heals, then ask if it's okay to pray for them. Again, what have you got to lose?

Be Bold!

If you are bold, you might end up with a great testimony and leading someone to Jesus. Now, a bit of a caution. During church services, make sure you operate properly under the authority of your pastor by asking if they have a prayer team you could join.

I find that in the American church, the idea of healing is rather foreign, so I feel fortunate to have experienced many miraculous healings. I witnessed my first healing, as my mentor, Tim, began throwing up blood one day and was rushed to the hospital. At first the doctors thought it was a bleeding ulcer, but it turned out to be a rupture and he was bleeding out. Tim remembers the doctors saying, "We're losing him" to which he replied, "I will live and not die, by Jesus' stripes I am healed." Two weeks later, he was back teaching a session of Discipleship Training School and for the first time, I realized that God is still in the healing business.

Healing is Still for Today

I've been part of groups that prayed over people with heart issues, broken bones, just about every type of disease including cancer, and have witnessed many documented healings. We prayed over one man who had lived a hard life of alcohol and drugs. Although he was in his late twenties, the doctor told him he had the heart of a 60-year-old and there was severe damage, requiring multiple surgeries. He had exams and written medical reports to prove the damage and medical needs. We laid hands on him, anointed him with oil and prayed that God would give him a new heart. A week later, when he went back to the doctor, they could find no signs of damage and told him he had the heart of a 20-year-old. He had the medical reports to document the healing.

Another member of our church stepped off a curb wrong and hurt her ankle. At the emergency room, the x-rays showed a severe break, which was going to require surgery and a long recovery time. She came to the church in a boot. We laid hands on her, anointed her with oil, and prayed. When she went to the appointment with the orthopedic surgeon, they did another set of x-rays and found no break.

I've personally experienced many healings. In fact, I'm convinced that God has saved my life several times. On one occasion, I was experiencing severe stomach pain and Karen laid hands on my stomach and prayed. The pain immediately left and didn't return. Another time, I had an allergic reaction to something I ate, and my throat began to close. I couldn't breathe and thought that my time was up, but a friend acted quickly in prayer and my airway immediately opened.

Some of my healings have been instantaneous and others have taken time to manifest. One such case was a large bump on the inner white part of my left eye. It didn't hurt or bother me, but people could see it and would ask about it. I prayed and had people pray, but there was no change. I continued to believe and speak that it was healed and three years later I looked in the mirror one morning and it was gone.

Tumor Disappears

One of my favorite healing stories was told by a friend of mine about his wife. She had been diagnosed with a stomach tumor. My friend and other true disciples laid hands on her and prayed, and she believed she was healed. Prior to surgery, she was to have a CT scan of her stomach to determine the size and exact location. She proceeded to tell all the people at the office that God had healed her, and the tumor wouldn't be there.

All the medical staff were polite, but it was easy to see they didn't believe. When they put her in for the scan, they literally watched it shrink and disappear on the screen. She said, "I told you God was going to heal me" and some of them believed.

God is still in the healing business and we, as His true disciples, have been delegated authority over illness, disease, and injuries. If we step out in faith and speak in the powerful name of Jesus, we will see miracles happen.

There is another area of authority in Luke 8, when Jesus and the disciples were crossing a lake and encountered a sudden and severe storm. Jesus was sleeping in the boat and the disciples came to him in a panic. Here is the account from Luke 8:24 (NASB):

> *"They came to Jesus and woke Him up, saying, 'Master, Master, we are perishing!' And He got up and rebuked the wind and the surging waves, and they stopped, and it became calm."*

Clearly Jesus had authority to stop a storm and from his next comment (v. 25), *"Where is your faith?"*, Jesus expected his disciples to do the same.

As I was growing in my faith, I began recognizing that Jesus expected his disciples to operate with the same authority he did. It really connected when I read that Jesus did nothing on his own. I began to believe that if Jesus could rebuke a storm, so could any believer who was operating in faith.

Authority Over Weather

The authority over weather was tested one day in Washington state. A friend and I were driving to an ocean retreat and decided to play a round of golf on the way to the retreat destination. The only trouble was that it started raining and was pouring rain all the way to the golf course. We rose up in faith and began rebuking the storm. As we pulled into the parking lot at the golf course, the rain stopped, and clouds cleared. We played 9 holes of golf in sunshine. As we drove out of the parking lot, it began to rain again and poured rain for the next hour and a half as we drove to the retreat.

The next day at the retreat, there was a mix up and we

didn't have a meeting room. It was raining outside, but our faith had been strengthened the prior day, so my friend and I once again rose up in faith and rebuked the storm. It cleared off and we enjoyed several hours of sunshine and were able to have the meeting outside.

There have been many other times when I've rebuked storms and had them stop or move away from where I was. Recently, Karen and I heard on the news that a large dust storm was approaching our house in the Phoenix area. I went to the back yard and rebuked the storm. It made a hard-right turn and completely missed us. Even the news reported the strange change of direction.

It's God, Not Me

I'd love to say that my success with rebuking storms was 100%, but if that were the case then when we lived in Tacoma, Washington, it would have been the sunniest place on earth (and it definitely wasn't). God is still the one doing the work, so it's always His will, not ours. The key is to be willing to step out in faith and use the authority that Jesus gave his true disciples.

From the various stories in the Bible and my own personal experiences there seem to be keys to operating in authority:

1. Only true disciples (those who have picked up the cross and are following Jesus and not just sitting in a weekly church service) have been given authority.
2. They must have the faith necessary to step out and operate with authority when opportunities arise, and they are prompted by the Holy Spirit.
3. They must speak. Proverbs 18:21 says that the tongue carries the power of life and death. Our words carry authority, so be careful what you say to yourself, others, and about circumstances. They aren't just words and they can hurt.

ROD NICHOLS

Now, a few of quick cautions about authority, because it can really go to your head and cause pride. First, remember that it's delegated power, so it's never you doing anything. Second, although we have authority over many things on the earth and over the demonic realm, we do not have authority over other human beings. We can speak with authority when someone is either possessed by a demon (as Jesus and Paul did) or motivated by a demonic presence, but God has given each person a free will and we have no authority over a person's will.

Jesus received full authority in this world, and he passed it on to his true disciples. He expects us to operate with that authority, so that our world can become more like heaven. As a true disciple, it's time to get out of the pew or chair and start walking in your authority.

END NOTES

1. Kenneth Hagin Ministries; 2nd edition (December 1, 1985)
2. Saints Who Raised the Dead: The True Story of 400 Resurrection Miracles. TAN Books, January 1, 1986.
3. https://www.charismamag.com/blogs/the-strang-report/40981-i-died-an-unbeliever-boy-who-came-back-to-life-after-an-hour-shares-details-of-his-resurrection
4. Raising the Dead: A Doctor Encounters the Miraculous. Faith Words, March 28, 2012.
5. 90 Minutes in Heaven. Revell, July 1, 2014.

Discussion for Chapter 8: Authority

1. Discuss what authority means in the life of a believer.

2. Talk about resurrection and any fears around praying for someone to come back from the dead.

3. Share any faith-based healing experiences you've had.

4. Discuss any fears you have about praying for sick, injured, or handicapped people.

CHAPTER NINE

✝

FASTING

Prior to launching our first church in 2001, we experienced many spiritual retreats and that was when I was introduced to the power of fasting. Now, first I need you to know that I love food and the idea of giving it up for a period of time (even one meal), was not appealing at all. However, I was committed enough to my walk, that I was willing to give it a try.

My mentor, Tim, taught on fasting and showed us how Jesus had instructed his disciples to fast. He even told them that some prayers could only be answered with fasting added (Matthew 17:21 NASB). I started with a 3-day fast and it wasn't too bad. That progressed to a few 10-day fasts, followed by a couple for 21 days, and then three 40-day fasts.

There is no question that fasting food will cause you to pray more, because you feel like your starving (ha, ha), but seriously, it will draw you closer to the Lord. We often fasted in the days leading up to our retreats and because we were so sensitive to the Lord's voice, our prayer times were powerful and as close to heaven on earth, as I've experienced. If you want to learn more about fasting, read, *The Hidden Power of Prayer and Fasting*, by Mahesh Chavda[1], as it was the book that guided us at that time. More recently, we have read *Fasting* by Jentezen Franklin[2], which is another excellent resource for those interested in the power of fasting.

Fasting was a big part of our first church plant. Our planting group of thirteen people had already experienced many fasts and spiritual retreats leading up to launching the church on January 14, 2001. We held services in a small coffee shop for the first three weeks, but quickly had over thirty in attendance and were in need of a bigger building.

Fasting and Praying for a New Building

We began fasting and praying and the Lord led us to an office building that had two large office spaces with a foyer and restrooms in between. They were asking $2400 per month for one half of the building, which was a long way from our budget of $1000, so we continued fasting and praying. We sensed that the Lord wanted us to offer $1,000 per month with an additional $100 each month until we reached the $2400. They accepted, and we had a 2000 square foot office with a large open area for the sanctuary and three small offices.

That was great, except that we didn't have any furniture. We needed at least thirty chairs and a small sound system within a week. Again, through prayer and fasting, God provided the chairs, sound system, desks, computers, tables, and more. We continued to utilize that building for a little under two years, but our children's ministry had taken over the offices and we were bursting at the seams. We needed more space.

We had approached the Attorney on the other side of the building several times, but he was not planning to move. Again, we began fasting and praying and within a few days, the Attorney approached us about taking over the space, because he was moving. He even offered the space at less than he was paying for the balance of his contract, so that he could move right away. The Lord then brought in $10,000 to cover the remodeling necessary, so we could move our children's ministry to that side of the building.

A year or so later, we were two months away from the end of our lease for that building and were again in need of more space. For about six months we had been hunting for space, but there was just nothing that fit our size requirements and budget, so Pastor Tim called for a 40 day fast and weekly prayer times.

Eyes Wide Open

One day I was driving through the area where my family lived and noticed that a small grocery store that had been there for years was gone. I inquired about the space and it was available. They were even willing to do some build out. We ended up doubling our space for a fraction more than we were currently paying and there was room within the building to grow.

I'm sure it's easy to see that I'm a big believer in the power of fasting and encourage all true disciples to fast and pray.

Let's jump back to the Bible and see what it has to say about fasting. Jesus' first act in ministry was a 40 day fast (Matthew 4:1-2). That's right, he went without food for 40 days. If you are anything like I was in my early days of walking with the Lord, you can't imagine going a day without food, much less 40 days. Yet, under the inspiration of the Holy Spirit, that's exactly what he did.

Jesus wasn't the first in the Bible to fast 40 days. Moses did it twice (Exodus 24:18, 34:28). Moses and Jesus are two of God's most powerful figures in history. I think perhaps there is a correlation, between power and fasting.

In Matthew 6:16-18, Jesus taught his disciples about fasting. The beginning of verse 16 reads, *"When you fast."* Clearly, Jesus expected his true disciples to fast. He goes on to say that we aren't to make a big show of it. In fact, we should act normal, so that no one would ever know that we are fasting. Again, as with prayer, God rewards what is done in secret.

We see several types of fasts in the Bible. Daniel fasted for three weeks (Daniel 10:2-3), during which he ate no choice food or meat and did not drink wine. The New Living Translation says that Daniel ate no rich foods. The Message Bible (paraphrase) says that Daniel ate only plain and simple foods. Most Bible scholars believe he was eating vegetables, nuts, and drinking only water (this is based on comments in Daniel 1:12). Now, it also says that he neither bathed nor shaved and unless you are unemployed and not married, I would not recommend this part. Let's just stick with the minimal food and water.

It's the Why That Matters

What you fast, is not quite as important as why you fast. First, it's not a diet and this type of fasting is not for weight loss. That may be a bi-product of a longer fast (21 to 40 days), but it should not be the reason. You are fasting as a spiritual commitment to the Lord. Take the time you would typically use to prepare and eat meals to meditate in the Word and pray.

Fasting food and drinks is a challenge to the flesh and there will be objections. This is a good opportunity to crucify the flesh with its passions and desires (Galatians 5:24). The more you crucify the flesh, the more open you will be to the Holy Spirit. That's why people rave about how close they feel to the Lord after a 21 or 40 day fast.

Again, the length of the fast is not as important as the purpose for the fast. In God's realm there is no time, so He doesn't care if your fast is 1 or 40 days. That said, it does make a difference in your connection with God, so perhaps start with a 1 day fast, then move to 3, 10, 21, and 40. Since I was always working during my fasts, I would do liquid only fasts and drink protein drinks to keep up my energy and a sharp mind. The idea is not to starve yourself, but to crucify the flesh and increase connection with the Holy Spirit.

A Caution About Fasting

Now, a bit of a caution. In Exodus 34:28 we see that Moses was up on the mountain of God for 40 days and he ate no bread and drank no water. Unless God specifically tells you to go without food and water for 40 days, don't do it. The only reason Moses could do this was that he was in the literal presence of the Lord. I know some who have done 40-day water only fasts and again, this should be done under the instruction and inspiration of the Holy Spirit.

I've completed three 40-day fasts, but they have all included lots of water, juices and protein drinks, so I could continue to think and work. For one 40-day fast, I only drank liquid for the first 10 days, a Daniel fast the next 20, and liquid only the final 10 days.

All of these fasts were powerful and drew me into a closer, more intimate relationship with the Lord. I also received revelation for books, ministries, and businesses during those fasts.

If you have health issues that a fast could exacerbate, check with your Doctor prior to starting a fast. Also, pray that during the fast, God will heal your health issue.

Fasting, when combined with prayer, faith, and authority can be very powerful. After fasts, I've experienced many miraculous times.

Jesus told his disciples to fast, so if you are a true disciple, you will fast.

END NOTES

1. The Hidden Power of Prayer and Fasting. Destiny Image Publishers, January 1, 2007.
2. Fasting. Charisma House, December 14, 2007.

Discussion for Chapter 9: Fasting

1. Why did Jesus tell his disciples (that's us) to fast?

2. Discuss your experiences with fasting.

3. Share any fears you have about fasting.

4. Commit to a fast within the next month and share that with the group.

CHAPTER TEN

†

SERVING

I spent many years in sports, working to be the best and to win. Then I moved into the business world with the same goals. It was all about me and being #1. This programming resulted in a selfish "me" focus. As the best, I expected preferential treatment and when I didn't get what I thought I deserved, I got angry. This attitude ruined many friendships, business relationships, ministries, and my first marriage. It almost ruined my current marriage.

Many people have this selfish approach and this attitude is causing dissension in every aspect of life, including friendships and marriages. Selfishness is even splitting and destroying churches and ministries. Obviously, this is not the way a true disciple should act.

When I became a Jesus follower, I discovered a new approach to life. Jesus told His disciples that He didn't come to be served, but to serve; to give His life as a ransom for many (Mark 10:45). That's a bit mind blowing, as Jesus is the Word, who spoke everything into existence. He is the Alpha and Omega. He is the King of Kings and Lord of Lords. Yet, he didn't expect to be served; he chose to serve.

Jesus was the ultimate servant and a model for His true disciples.

To begin, let's define servant. Dictionary.com has three definitions and the one that fits best here is, "a person in service of another". The Greek word that is translated as "serve" in Mark 10:45 is diakoneo, which is where we get our word deacon. It means to minister to one or render ministry; to provide for or take care of someone; to serve another's interests.

In the days of Jesus and the disciples, wealthy homes had servants who did the menial work. The lowest of servants would wash the feet of the master, his family, and guests. Unlike our world today, they walked on dirt/mud roads covered in animal excrement. They didn't take nice hot showers every day and put lotion on their feet. They didn't have metal toenail clippers or get pedicures. They also didn't wear nice shoes; they wore sandals. These were dirty, smelly, and gnarly feet. Cleaning them was not the job anyone wanted to have.

Yet, as accounted in John 13:5-11, Jesus takes off his priestly robe, kneels and washes the feet of His disciples. Here is the Son of God, one of the Godhead, who prior to his birth as a human baby, was basking in the permanent glory of God, taking on the role of the lowest of servants.

Jesus Wants Us to Serve

As Jesus often did, he was using an illustrated sermon. It's not that he wanted the disciples to go around washing feet, rather he wanted them to take on the attitude of a servant. No part of ministry was too low or beneath them. In the church today, this might be the senior pastor of a megachurch taking off his suit to scrub the toilets and bathroom floors in a slum house.

In another account (Mark 9:34-35), the disciples had been arguing about who would be the greatest in the new

Kingdom. In Matthew's version (Matthew 20:20-28), the mother of the sons of Zebedee (John and James) came to Jesus and asked him to allow her sons to sit to the right and left (seats of honor) in His Kingdom. In both accounts, Jesus responded by telling them that if they wanted to be first in the Kingdom, they needed to become servants/slaves to all. In other words, they needed to give up their prideful, haughty attitude and start serving others.

In the beginning of Romans 1:1 (NASB), the Apostle Paul refers to himself as a bond-servant. *"Paul, a bond-servant of Christ Jesus, called as an apostle, set apart for the gospel of God."* (emphasis mine) In Luke, we see Simeon, a man the Bible calls *"righteous and devout"*. He had been waiting for the Messiah for many years and when he saw the child, Jesus, he said, *"Now Lord, You are releasing Your bond-servant to depart in peace."* [Luke 2:29, emphasis mine]

Bond-Servant

A bond-servant is defined as a person bound in service without wages. In other words, a slave. The Greek word used in Romans 1:1 and translated as bond-servant is Doulos, which means someone who gives himself in service to another or one who is subservient to another.

What is interesting about a bond-servant is that this person chooses to be a slave. Often slaves would be released and then choose to stay on as a bond-servant.

Jesus exemplified this bond-servant relationship. *"In the beginning was the Word, and the Word was with God, and the Word was God."* [John 1:1]. Imagine being in heaven on the day when the Word, chose or was asked to separate Himself from the God-head and be born as a human baby. WOW! He had to give up the glories of heaven, the omniscience (all knowing), omnipresence (all places at one time), omnipotence (all powerful), and the community of

ROD NICHOLS

heaven, to confine Himself in a human body.

The Word went from an eternal being who could never die to a human being who could die. He was confined to being in one place at a time, wasn't all powerful, and didn't know everything – Jesus had to rely on his connection with the Father, through the Holy Spirit (as we do). He chose to do this, because he loved us so much and because it would give joy to the Father.

In order for this to happen, the Word had to subjugate Himself to the Son role. In other words, He had to be placed subservient to the Father in heaven (Psalm 2:7) and then later, on earth (Matthew 3:17). Jesus was a bond-servant of the Father and he taught the disciples to be the same. This was how Paul came to use the terminology in Romans 1:1. As true disciples, we too are to become bond-servants of the Lord.

So, what does it mean to be a servant or bond-servant? Let's look at a few areas:

1. **God's will, not yours** – Jesus put the Father's will ahead of his own. This is evident in Luke 22:42: *"Father, if you are willing, take this cup from me; yet not my will, but yours be done."* We see the humanity of Jesus in this moment, when he is feeling the stress of what is to come. In verse 44, Dr. Luke describes a level of stress likely none of us has ever experienced. Jesus's sweat turns to blood. This is called Hematidrosis[1] and is a condition where the capillary blood vessels that feed the sweat glands rupture, causing them to exude blood. This only occurs under conditions of extreme physical or emotional stress. Even the man, Jesus, struggled with choosing God's will over his own.

We are His creation, made for Him (Colossians 1:16). We are God's masterpiece and we're made to do the good works He prepared in advance (Ephesians 2:10). You are not your own, you belong to God (1 Corinthians 6:19). If you are born again, your old selfish person should no longer make the decision, as Christ now lives in and through you (Galatians 2:20). We must do as Jesus did and say, "Lord, this is what I would like, but your will be done, not mine" in every situation. Servants always put the will of the Master before their own.

2. **Other's before self** – Again, Jesus gave us the example of putting the needs of others before his own. How often was he tired and tried to go off to a quiet place, only to be mobbed by people wanting healing and to hear what he had to say? He always put their needs before his own. This is contrary to sinful human nature. We are always looking out for #1, trying to get ahead at all cost, putting our own wants and needs before anyone else (including God). Philippians 2:3 (NLT) tells us *"don't be selfish; don't try to impress others. Be humble, thinking of others as better than yourselves"*. The NIV says to *"value others above yourselves"*. Romans 12:10 says that we are to *"honor one another above yourselves"* or *"give preference to one another in honor"* (NASB) or *"Excel at showing respect for each other"* (ISV). In every situation, we should be asking ourselves, What can I do to make someone else's life better/easier? We should be generous to others whenever we can. Jesus said that what we do for the *"least of these"* we do to him – feeding, clothing, housing, giving fresh water, love, money, and help. Every time you are putting someone else's needs before your own, imagine you are doing it for Jesus (because you are).

3. **Love** – When asked about the greatest commandment, Jesus responded, *"Love the Lord your God with all your heart and with all your soul and with all your mind. This is the first and greatest commandment. And the second is like it: Love your neighbor as yourself."* [Matthew 22:36-39]. As true disciples and bond-servants of God, we are to love

Him first, with everything we have and then love our neighbors (those around us) as we do ourselves. 1 Corinthians 13:4-8 shows us what this God-type of love looks like:

> *"Love is patient, love is kind. It does not envy, it does not boast, it is not proud. It does not dishonor others, it is not self-seeking, it is not easily angered, it keeps no record of wrongs. Love does not delight in evil but rejoices with the truth. It always protects, always trusts, always hopes, always perseveres. Love never fails."*

In God's eyes, love is not the emotion we see in the movies (and life), where people fall in and out of love. Love is a commitment to act in certain ways. Bond-servants love their Master, which is why they choose to stay in servitude to them. *"We love because He first loved us."*
[1 John 4:19]

4. **Willing to do the tough stuff for the benefit of others** - I'm sure Jesus didn't love the idea of being whipped 39 times with a lead tipped whip (John 19:1 NLT), which was a favorite tool of torture for the Roman soldiers. It was made up of a wood or metal handle with nine leather cords about 2-1/2 feet long. At the end of each cord was tied a piece of sharp metal, glass, or bone. The Romans were trained to draw the cords around the body and rip the flesh to the bone. Jesus received 39 lashes, which was the maximum allowed to ensure that the prisoner didn't die.

I'm sure Jesus didn't revel in the idea of carrying the rugged wooden cross beam on His back, which after the beating, probably looked like raw ground beef. I have no doubt that Jesus didn't enjoy the ridicule, being spit upon, struck upside the head, and having a crown with inch long thorns jammed into his skull.

I have no doubt that he did not enjoy having huge nails driven into his hands and feet. His human nature did not enjoy or want to do any of this, but *"for the joy set before him, he endured the cross, scorning its shame"* [Hebrews 12:2]. He did it for us, so we would not have to face the wrath of God and spend eternity tormented in hell. That's what bondservants do; they do the tough stuff for others.

The disciples/apostles all did it – in fact, all but John died horrendous deaths, because they continued to preach the gospel and lead people to Christ. Paul was stoned so badly he was left for dead, yet he got up and kept preaching the gospel. Many people have given up their lives and freedom to spread the gospel of Jesus Christ. We must be willing to do the tough stuff for the benefit of others.

Put Your Spouse's Needs First

In your marriage, it means putting your spouse's wants and needs ahead of yours. At work, it means putting your boss's will before your own. In the church, it means putting the congregational needs before your own. As the greatest example of a servant, even when we were still his enemies, Jesus laid down his life for all of us. That's true love!

In our walk with the Lord it also means serving the *"least of these"*. Jesus addressed this in Matthew 25:35-40:

> *"For I was hungry and you gave me something to eat, I was thirsty and you gave me something to drink, I was a stranger and you invited me in, I needed clothes and you clothed me, I was sick and you looked after me, I was in prison and you came to visit me. Then the righteous will answer him, 'Lord, when did we see you hungry and feed you, or thirsty and give you something to drink? When did we see you a stranger and invite you in, or*

needing clothes and clothe you? When did we see you sick or in prison and go to visit you?' The King will reply, 'Truly I tell you, whatever you did for one of the least of these brothers and sisters of mine, you did for me.'"

This scripture is embedded in the middle of an end time description that starts in Chapter 24. In the prior verses (Matthew 25:31-33), Jesus is separating the goats (those who are not believers) to the left and sheep (those who are believers) to the right. He then speaks (Matthew 25:35-40) to the sheep on the right. Clearly, these believers had been feeding the hungry, giving water to the thirsty, inviting strangers into their home, taking care of the sick and visiting those in prison. Jesus then made it clear that when we do these things for other people, it's as if we are doing them for Jesus.

Not By Works

I struggled with this for some time, because the Bible tells us that salvation is through grace by faith (Ephesians 2:8-9), but this sounds like they are getting into heaven because they served. As I invested time studying this scripture, I realized that the serving was not the reason for the separation. They were separated because of their belief or lack of belief in Jesus, as Savior and Lord and how the Lord publicly recognized that was by their servant's heart.

Before we are born-again, we are selfish and self-focused. We serve if there is some personal benefit, not because we are driven to serve. As we saw earlier, although Jesus was the Son of God and deserved to be served, He did not come to be served, but to serve. Since we have the Spirit of Jesus Christ (Philippians 1:19), we have that heart of a servant inside of us. As our mind, will and emotions are transformed by the Word of God, we will feel driven to serve. We have the heart and mind of Christ, as we look upon the least of these.

This is exactly what happened to me. I was about as selfish and self-focused as they come. In fact, I came into the Kingdom kicking and screaming. The Hound of Heaven had to drag me in by the leg. I wish I could say that I was immediately transformed into an amazing servant, but I wasn't. In fact, I began serving like a pagan – finding ways that I could serve to gain recognition or meet the right people. It wasn't until I was roped into doing a street outreach that my hard heart broke for the least of these.

This breaking continued through the years, as we had opportunities to deliver Thanksgiving meals to people in need. I would help take boxes or bags of food into the homes and was always surprised at the lack of furniture and the shape of the home. One of the best Christmases ever was when we adopted a single Mom and her three children. We supplied a tree, decorations, lights, a Christmas meal, presents for her and gifts she could give to her children. The smiles on the children's faces, as we set up the tree and the tears in the mother's eyes were heart wrenching.

Feeding the Poor

As time went on, we continued our service through a feeding outreach in an isolated and very low-income area south of Tacoma, Washington. Every Wednesday, we would pull in a 26' truck and hand out packaged foods, bread, fruit, and produce to people from the community. At first, they wouldn't even look us in the eyes, but we just kept loving on them and soon we had friends.

This expanded into a monthly hot meal with prize giveaways, backpacks with school supplies, Christmas gifts for the kids, and filling many other needs. We didn't need to preach the gospel verbally, they felt it in our service. In fact, quite often people would come and just hang around.

They didn't need food, but they liked being around our team. It was the light of the Servant inside us that attracted them.

When God called us to move to Arizona, He provided a full circle moment, as the church we turned the ministry over to was planted out of the church where we were saved many years prior. They took the outreach ministry to new heights by expanding the hot meal to weekly, moving team members into the neighborhood and doing weekly Bible studies, running busses to the services on Sunday, and plans to bring in a mobile dental and medical clinic. It's been heart- warming to see the area and people changed over time.

True disciples of Jesus are just like him, servants!

END NOTE

1. https://www.healthline.com/health/hematidrosis

Discussion for Chapter 10: Serving

1. Share how you are currently serving in your life.

2. Discuss how you could serve more in your family.

3. Talk about how you could serve more at work.

4. What are some ways you could serve more at church?

CHAPTER ELEVEN

†

PREACHING

In Mark 16:15, Jesus told his disciples, *"Go into all the world and preach the gospel to all creation."* The gospel is the good news about Jesus' sacrifice for our sin and our opportunity to receive the gift of grace, so that we can not only walk with the Holy Spirit inside us here on earth, but spend eternity with God and other believers in the new heaven on earth (Revelation 21:1-2).

If you are like I was early in my walk with the Lord, you may think preaching is what the pastor or minister does in front of the church on Sunday morning. I thought they were the only people who "preached" and yet, Jesus told his disciples to go and preach. That baffled me for several years, until I learned how to rightly divide the Word of God (2 Timothy 2:15 KJV). By using an interlinear online Bible (just do a Google search for Interlinear Bible or download an app), entering Mark 16:15, and then clicking on the word "preach", I discovered that it means to be a herald or to proclaim in the manner of a herald. The problem is that we don't have heralds today. In the days before the phones, television, radio, and internet, when the king wanted to tell his people something, he would send out a herald – "Hear Ye, Hear Ye, by the order of the king..." It was a public proclamation from the king.

Jesus was teaching his disciples that the King (Jesus) wanted his people to be heralds for the Kingdom. They were to go out to all parts of the world and tell what had happened – how they had spent time with Jesus, watched him heal people and drive out demons, then how he went to the cross and died a gruesome death to forgive the sins of all mankind for all time. Then they were to tell how Jesus was resurrected, appeared to people for 40 days, was taken into heaven and now sits at the right hand of the Father. Finally, they were to tell how they were in the upper room praying and the Holy Spirit fell on them and they were baptized with the Holy Spirit and fire (which John the Baptist had predicted in Matthew 3:11).

Eye Witness Accounts

Okay, so I know what you're thinking. You weren't there walking with Jesus; didn't see him heal and deliver; didn't watch him die on the cross and appear in his resurrected body; didn't see him ascend into heaven; and you weren't there in the upper room getting baptized with the Holy Spirit and fire.

The good news is that your Bible is filled with eye witness accounts. Jesus expects his true disciples to believe these accounts and begin "preaching" the good news about Jesus and salvation.

Preaching is not just standing in a pulpit or on a platform at church on Sunday morning. It's telling your story about how you found Jesus (or how he found you) and how your life is different – it's called a testimony. In fact, Jesus told the disciples to wait in Jerusalem for the arrival of the Holy Spirit and said, *"But you will receive power when the Holy Spirit comes on you; and you will be my witnesses in Jerusalem, and in all Judea and Samaria, and to the ends of the earth."* [Acts 1:8].

In a trial, what does a witness do? They tell what they saw, heard, and experienced – it's called testimony. That's what Jesus calls his disciples to do – give your testimony – what was your life like before you turned it over to Jesus and what is it like now? How has your future hope changed, now that you know that you are going to spend eternity in the glories of heaven with God and all the saints? Develop your story, so you can give a short version – in the time it would take to ride up or down a couple floors in an elevator and a longer version – maybe 5 to 10 minutes that you could share over coffee or in a group setting.

Your Testimony is Preaching

Preaching doesn't always have to be about salvation. Some people just need to hear how Jesus has changed your life. Think about what your life was like before you accepted Jesus as your Savior. Were you selfish, self-focused, angry, addicted, foul mouthed, lazy, or greedy? Did you lie, cheat, or steal? Did you lust after men or women? Have you had an affair or an abortion? If Jesus has changed you, then these areas of change are the seeds of a great testimony. One that will give others hope that their life can change.

I have shared my very transparent testimony of God's transformation many times with individuals and groups. I can recall so many times, when I've shared about my problem with anger and how I would punch holes in walls and break things, and the person would say, "I just can't imagine you like that." It ministered hope that their life could change, as well.

Many times, Karen and I have shared our marriage testimony. How we used to fight and scream obscenities at each other. Couples see us now as a loving married couple and they can't imagine us acting like that. Again, it ministers hope for their marriage.

Working with men who struggle with sexual addiction, my testimony of God delivering me has ministered to hundreds of men. It's that hope of freedom that opens the door for the Holy Spirit to begin working in their lives and *"where the Spirit of the Lord is, there is freedom."* [2 Corinthians 3:17].

Here's the reason why I find most people struggle sharing their testimony – pride. You have to admit that you've done bad things. There might also be some shame still attached and you are afraid of what people will think of you. There may be some people in your life who react badly, but that's their problem, not yours. Jesus took all your shame and left it on the cross. God loves you and wants you to transparently share your transformation story. It will help those who hear it move closer to God, their own personal transformation and salvation.

No Testimony?

Perhaps you're thinking that you grew up in the church, in a Christian family and you've never done anything bad. I remember Tim, my spiritual mentor, telling me that one day. He used to say he was practically born in the pew. His parents were wonderful Christian people and Tim was raised in the church. He then went to Bible college and right into ministry. He has a fantastic story of God's grace and I told him that I would love to have his testimony. It would have saved me a lot of pain and heartache. So, if you are like Tim, you still need to be preaching what God has done in your life.

Testimonials are not just words that you share with others. You can also testify through your actions. Jesus teaches this in Matthew 5:16:

"In the same way, let your light shine before others, that they may see your good deeds and glorify your Father in heaven."

I always share in my testimony that our oldest daughter was the light that brought salvation into our home. It wasn't through her words, but rather through the changes we saw in her life. Karen noticed and followed her into church and re-committed her life to the Lord. I then saw the changes in Karen's life, and it opened me to the draw of the Holy Spirit.

Karen was a perfect example of what the Apostle Peter says in 1 Peter 3:1-2:

"Wives, in the same way submit yourselves to your own husbands so that, if any of them do not believe the word, they may be won over without words by the behavior of their wives, when they see the purity and reverence of your lives."

Even though I was not following Jesus, Karen submitted to me as her husband. She didn't preach (in the negative way) about Jesus. Instead, she just let her behavior speak loudly. I noticed that she wasn't getting as angry and seemed to have more peace. I also noticed her reverence for Jesus and the Word of God. Mostly, I noticed that she had more joy. I wanted all of that and it caused me to begin to seek.

There are many people out there just like me. They just need someone to come along and preach through words and/or actions. One of the favorite testimonial stories I've read is about the salvation of the Stephen Baldwin family. Stephen's wife, Kennya is Brazilian, and they hired a Brazilian nanny to take care of the kids and clean the house. As the nanny was cleaning, she would sing in Portuguese. Stephen's wife began listening and realized that the nanny was singing about Jesus. Kennya reported this to Stephen, who didn't really care. He had grown up Catholic and left the faith. However, the singing peaked Kennya's interest and she began talking with the nanny about Jesus. This led to her salvation. Similar to my story, Stephen noticed the changes in Kennya and even referred to her as a "Jesus freak". After the devastation of 9-11, as many people did, Stephen began thinking about faith, pursued it and was born again. All because of a nanny who preached through her singing[1].

Radical Salvation

I've encountered many Christians who had lived a hard-partying lifestyle and then experienced a radical salvation where they completely gave up that way of life. All their partying friends noticed the sudden change and began asking, which opened the door for a conversation about Jesus. This is another great example of preaching. First was the action and then the words.

Some people will be called to preach in church services, others will be called into the mission field to preach to those who may have never even heard of Jesus. Most will work at jobs or own businesses and raise families, but they are still called to preach the good news of Jesus through words and actions.

As a true disciple of Jesus Christ, you are called to preach the gospel to the world (or at least to the world around you).

END NOTE

1. http://godreports.com/2017/03/brazilian-nanny-led-actor-stephen-baldwin-and-wife-to-the-lord-by-singing-about-jesus-to-their-baby/

Discussion for Chapter 11: Preaching

1. Discuss what has stopped you from sharing the gospel with others.

2. Share if you have received a call from God to preach the gospel and the status of that calling.

3. Talk about some positive or negative experiences you've had preaching the gospel and what you learned.

4. Share a personal testimony or one you remember that impacted your life.

CHAPTER TWELVE

✝

LOVING

I remember, as a seven-year old, falling in love with baseball. I loved to watch and play the game. I loved the smell of the dirt and the feel of the ball smacking into my mitt. The sound of a solid hit off a wood bat was music to my ears. The satisfaction of completing a hook slide to the outside of second base and hearing the umpire yell, "SAFE", was the best. I dreamed, as many boys do, of standing in the batter's box with runners on base, down by a run in the bottom of the 9th of the seventh game of the World Series and hitting a grand slam. Baseball was the love of my life for many years, until I got interested in girls and then it was a very high second place.

Speaking of girls, I kissed the first one in Kindergarten and got in big trouble. My first infatuation was when I was twelve, but that one didn't work out either. Since my love of baseball was so strong and I was a very shy kid with a questionable self-image, I didn't start dating until my senior year of high school. I started late but fell hard. When I was with my first real girlfriend, it felt like what I thought heaven might feel like. When we parted, the pain was

127

agonizing. Sappy young love. That one didn't work out either, as she dumped me a week before Senior Prom.

Today, I am married to and madly in love with Karen, my wife of over thirty years. She is my soul mate, by best friend, lover, and life mate. As you can tell, from this book, we have been through a lot together. She has stuck with me during the good, the bad, and the ugly. When I read about the Proverbs 31 woman, I see Karen. I give thanks every day that God allowed me to have such an amazing wife. She is the love of my life.

So why am I talking about the loves of my life? Because that's what people typically think of when the topic of love arises. They love their spouse, children, parents, relatives, house, job, business, vacation, car, pool, boat, money, clothes, jewelry, and so on. We do love our stuff, don't we? But, that's not what this chapter is all about.

At the last supper, as Jesus was preparing for his betrayal, capture, torture, and death, he said to the disciples:

> *"So now I am giving you a new commandment: Love each other. Just as I have loved you, you should love each other. Your love for one another will prove to the world that you are my disciples."*
> [John 13:34-35 NLT]

We aren't known as true disciples by our good works, by amazing preaching, by the number of people who attend church services, by the amount of money we raise for missions, by the mission trips we take, or by the number of people we lead to the Lord. They aren't even going to know us by the signs and wonders that follow us. They will know that we are true disciples of Jesus by our love for other believers.

Jesus wasn't talking about the emotional love we see in the world, where people love their people, pets, and stuff.

No, Jesus was referencing the kind of love that God has for His people. We find that type of love in 1 Corinthians 13:4-8:

> *"Love is patient, love is kind. It does not envy, it does not boast, it is not proud. It does not dishonor others, it is not self-seeking, it is not easily angered, it keeps no record of wrongs. Love does not delight in evil but rejoices with the truth. It always protects, always trusts, always hopes, always perseveres. Love never fails."*

Let's break this scripture down, so that we know how to love one another:

1. Love is Patient – The King James Version uses "long suffering" and the New King James Version uses, "suffers long" instead of patient, which I think are better translations for that word. In our fast-paced world, we think patience is waiting the minute or so to get our food out of the microwave. This is not the type of patience God is talking about.

The Greek word translated as patient is *makrothumeo* and it means not to lose heart during trying times; enduring offenses, misfortunes, and troubles. When loving others, this type of patience means that we don't get offended, we put up with their weaknesses; we don't take to heart their negative words or actions, we endure through times of strained relationship; and we also seek to stay in relationship. We learn to live and work together with our differences. Love is willing to suffer long, when necessary. With all my struggles, Karen, my wife, has shown this part of love time and time again. She is a great example of someone who loves patiently.

2. Love is Kind – This one is a little easier, because all the versions use "kind" and it's the right word. If you have parents, a spouse, children, or friends (which of course, is all of us) you have probably at times not been kind. You might have said hurtful things, posted mean things on social media, tweeted something unkind, or just ignored the person for a period of time. This is how love works in the world, but in God's Kingdom, love is ALWAYS kind. The key here is that to show ourselves as true disciples of Jesus, we are to show kindness to all people – everywhere!

In the front of our mind should be thoughts of how we can show kindness to each other. My spiritual mentor, Tim Johnson, once showed his love for Karen and me by spearheading a project to replace a rotten deck at our house, so we could sell the home. He paid for the wood and brought in a group of people, who also showed their love for us by working a couple days to tear down the old deck and build a beautiful new one. That's loving one another and has been a great example to many people, as I've shared the story.

3. **Love Does Not Envy** – So, how does it feel, when you've been pressing in for a financial breakthrough and someone else receives a big promotion or financial blessing? How have you responded, when you've struggled with your health and others were receiving healing. How about when you attended a meeting of pastors or leaders and your church was the smallest? What about when someone in the church gets a brand-new car and yours is held together by duct tape? If you weren't celebrating with the others for their victory, then you were operating in envy. Have you compared your house to another and wished you had the bigger, better one? What about that perfect spouse your best Christian friend has – have you wished your spouse was more like him/her? That also is envy.

The God kind of love does not envy, it rejoices in the

successes of others and is content with what God gives. 1 Corinthians 12:26 (NASB) says of the body of Christ, "*if one member is honored, all the members rejoice*". This is counter to the way the world works. If you are struggling and yet continue to rejoice in what God has provided for you or any other believer, people will notice and remember that you walk with Jesus.

4. Love Does Not Boast and is Not Proud – So many people in the world boast or brag about their successful lives. They brag about houses, cars, trips, business success, awards, private schools their children attend, and so on. This can cause others to feel left out, inadequate, unfortunate, forgotten, and sad. People who are operating in the God kind of love never boast, because they know that all of it comes from God and that except for with God, they can do and have nothing good.

Proverbs 16:18 says, "*Pride goes before destruction, a haughty (proud) spirit before a fall.*" (emphasis mine) Unfortunately, it's this pride that keeps many people from loving God and receiving Christ and so they die with the most toys and end up spending eternity tormented in hell. That's a big fall. I know several believers who have achieved a high level of success in life and yet you would never know it by the way they talk or act. A true disciple knows how to love.

5. Love Does Not Dishonor Others – Have you ever talked badly about another believer to someone else when they weren't there? That's dishonoring them. Have you spoken negatively of a TV preacher? That's dishonoring them. Have you ever lied to or cheated someone? That's dishonoring them. These are the kinds of things people of the world do. It's the norm in our society, but in God's Kingdom, as true disciples, we don't dishonor others. In fact, we are to think of them as more valuable than ourselves and honor them in every opportunity. People will recognize that we are true disciples of Jesus by how often we honor each other.

6. **Love is Not Self-Seeking** – Worldly love is very self-focused and it's the reason that there are so many divorces. Unfortunately, Christian couples can also love in the worldly way, which again, is why there are so many Christian divorces. God's type of love is the opposite – it's other's focused. This type of love focuses on the wants and needs of the other, putting them before self.

Our love for fellow believers needs to be selfless and others focused. 1 Corinthians 10:24 says, *"No one should seek their own good, but the good of others."* Philippians 2:3-4 extends the concept, *"Do nothing out of selfish ambition or vain conceit. Rather, in humility value others above yourselves, not looking to your own interests but each of you to the interests of the others."*

Jesus showed this type of love, when he gave up the glories of heaven and his godly attributes to be born a human baby and then gave up his life to redeem our sins. That's true love. John 15:13 (NLT) says it best, *"There is no greater love than to lay down one's life for one's friends."* Now, you don't have to literally lay down your life, as Jesus did, but you do need to lay down that selfish flesh and let the Spirit love through you!

7. **Love is Not Easily Angered** – In relationships that are relying on worldly love, there is anger and arguments, unforgiveness, and even domestic violence. This type of love is based on feelings and feelings change with the circumstances. The God-type of love is only based on God and He never changes.

Karen and I weren't saved for the first 10 years of our relationship and so all we knew was the worldly kind of love. We always said that we were passionate in our loving and our fighting, as there were times when we were both easily angered. Fortunately, since we accepted Jesus and learned to walk in the Spirit, the fights have been few and far between and very little anger.

This applies to all types of relationships – friends, family, work, church, neighbors. People will do and say stupid things that will prompt us to be angry. If you are full of God's love, you are less likely to get angry. Learn to love people with the God-type of love and life will be so much more peaceful and quieter.

8. **Love Keeps No Record of Wrongs** – Karen and I have often taken couples through pre-marital and marital coaching. One of the things we hear constantly is the list of things the other person has done wrong. It's not a written list, but it might as well be. That's the worldly kind of love. We've also seen family and friend relationships strained to the breaking point by those lists of wrongs.

True disciples, who operate in the God-type of love will quickly forgive and forget the wrongs of others. Bringing up all the things someone has done wrong will never have a positive result. Forget the wrongs and instead, start developing a list of all the things they do right and all that you love about them. Share that list with them often. That's what true disciples do.

9. **Love Does Not Delight in Evil but Rejoices with the Truth** – Satan and his army of fallen angels (demons) are constantly trying to destroy marriages. It's the easiest way to tear down the family structure, which is the foundation of our earthly life.

The enemy's plan for destruction does not extend just to marriages. It's also aimed at family, church, business, and community relationships. Satan delights in causing division through gossip, lying, cheating, and stealing. Can't imagine letting the devil do this in your life? How about the last time you were at church – did you complain about anything to your spouse or a friend? Maybe, they didn't play the songs you like best or the music was too loud, or the pastor didn't feed you during the message? Perhaps, someone busily passed you without acknowledging you, did you get offended? What about that offering message – did you have a thought that the church is always asking for money? The enemy is sly and will slip into your thoughts when you least expect it.

Believers must be careful not to listen to the lies of the enemy; not to delight in evil thoughts or actions. Instead, this God-love rejoices in the truth of God's Word. It honors those who love and are loved this way. Keep God in the center of every relationship (including the church) and you will always rejoice in the truth.

10. **Love Always Protects** – If there were a knock at the front door and through the peephole you could see a group of heavily armed thugs, would you open the door and say, "have your way with my spouse and family"? Of course not. No one in their right mind would do that and yet Christians do that every day when they look at pornography, read smutty novels, watch sleazy and violent programs or movies, fantasize about what it would be like to be with someone else, speak negatively, lie to and deceive each other, or get angry. This opens the door for the enemy to steal, kill, and destroy within your relationships.

This is not just the case with sexual sin; sin of any kind – lying, stealing, gossiping, envying, coveting, greed, and so on – opens the door for the enemy's army to attack you, your family, finances, and health. If you're a church pastor or leader, sin impacts your congregation and the health of your church. If you love your family and church, you must not open the door with deliberate sin.

So, stay in the Word of God, pray, ask the Lord to keep

you from sin and guide you to love in the same way He does, and your love will always protect.

11. **Love Always Trusts** – The worldly type of love is not trustworthy, because it's based on human emotions, which cannot be trusted. It's why we see so much dishonesty portrayed in TV and movie relationships. It's normal for those worldly relationships, but not so for those who have given their lives to the Lord. You no longer love with worldly love, rather you love others with the love of God, which is always trustworthy. When I'm coaching couples, I tell them that they cannot trust their spouse. This results in the same shocked look that is probably on your face. I'm not telling them this because the spouse has done something un-trustworthy, but rather because no human being with a sin nature (which is everyone, except Jesus) can be trusted.

This concept holds true with any type of relationship. It's why in 2 Corinthians 6:14 Paul says, *"Do not be yoked together with unbelievers. For what do righteousness and wickedness have in common? Or what fellowship can light have with darkness?"* I've had business partnerships with non-believers and they never worked out. It's also important to be yoked equally with believers. I had a business relationship with another believer, but we were not equally yoked. He was a new believer, with a lot of the world still in him and I was a more mature in my walk with the Lord. I thought because we were both Christians, it would turn out great. It was a disaster of epic proportions that ended up costing me a lot of money.

The good news is that if your spouse or another person is a born-again Christian, you can trust the Jesus inside them, and that makes them trustworthy to the level of their relationship with Christ. So, as you enter any type of relationship, discern in the love of the Holy Spirit, how trustworthy this person is. Then, make sure you are letting the Holy Spirit discern and love through you.

12. **Love Always Hopes** – I've encountered many hopeless relationships. The worldly love (emotions) has died and now they can see no hope in regaining it (and they are correct). I'm sure that there had to be times when Jesus felt like the disciples were hopeless. How about when he had just finished telling them that he was going to be tortured and die; then he hears them arguing about who is going to be the greatest in his kingdom. I imagine Jesus slapping his forehead in frustration. On another occasion, the disciples were arguing with the religious leaders about a demon possessed boy. They asked Jesus why they couldn't cast out the demon and Jesus responded, *"You unbelieving generation," Jesus replied, 'how long shall I stay with you? How long shall I put up with you? Bring the boy to me.'"* (Mark 9:19) Jesus definitely had to love some seemingly hopeless people.

Psalm 31:24 (NKJV) says:

"Be of good courage, And He shall strengthen your heart, All you who hope in the LORD."

Our hope is not in each other or some worldly emotion, it's in the Lord and the Lord is pure love, so there is always plenty of hope to go around. Get your eyes off the situation and on to Jesus and hope will return.

13. **Love Always Perseveres** – We live in a fallen world and even with God in the center of our relationships, there will still be difficult times. In John 16:33, Jesus tells us, *"In this world you will have trouble. But take heart! I have overcome the world."* Karen and I have experienced trouble – divorces, death of parents and siblings, bankruptcy, rebellious children, loss of jobs, business

failure, car repossession, health issues, surgery, and much more. In our BC (before Christ) days, we didn't handle these things well and even talked about getting divorced. That's because love was an emotion. Now that we have Jesus at the center of our relationship and lives, his love always perseveres.

If you are ever questioning whether the God kind of love perseveres, just think about what He had to persevere through to bring you into the Kingdom. For me, it was a lot. I was like Saul, the Christian hater, before he became Paul the Apostle. I spoke against God, made fun of the Bible, Christians, and church. I was angry and hurt people with my words. I stole, lied, sinned sexually and in about every other way. Yet, out of perfect love, He persevered, and I finally gave in and committed my life to Him. How about you? What did God have to persevere through to get you?

Whether it's your relationship with the Lord or other people, it's easy to give in when your love is an emotion, but when the love of Jesus flows through you, it will always persevere!

14. **Love Never Fails** – Worldly love will fail, but the God-type of love will never fail. Allow God to love through you and your relationships will be amazing.

Loving in this way is a daunting task, but it's how Jesus loves his true disciples and it's how a true disciple should love others. For this reason, Jesus said that the second greatest commandment (after loving God) was to love one another. We can't love each other, unless we first love God. So, if you're not doing well in the love department (and I'm not talking just about dating and marriage), then check your love relationship with God. A true disciple loves God and let's God love through him or her. That kind of love will never fail!

How much time are you spending with God each day? If

you're married, imagine what your relationship would be like, if you only spent that amount of time each day with your spouse. How about your job. What if you only spent a couple hours one day a week at work, what do you think would happen? There are many Christians who attend a church service for an hour or two once per week and that's the only time they spend with God. The more time spent with Him, the deeper your love will be and the more easily He can love through you.

Again, people are not going to recognize you as a true disciple by church attendance or your generosity or even by how much you serve. Paul illustrates this so perfectly in 1 Corinthians 13:1-3:

> *"If I speak in the tongues of men or of angels, but do not have love, I am only a resounding gong or a clanging cymbal. If I have the gift of prophecy and can fathom all mysteries and all knowledge, and if I have a faith that can move mountains, but do not have love, I am nothing. If I give all I possess to the poor and give over my body to hardship that I may boast, but do not have love, I gain nothing."*

Without the God-type of love, there is nothing we do that has any value, because if we aren't doing it in love, we are doing it for selfish reasons. One day, when we face the Lord, the things we have done and said will be submitted to holy fire and only those things done and said in love, will survive and result in reward.

In Matthew 7:21-23, Jesus is looking to the end times and addressing a group of people who believe they are Christians when he says:

> *"Not everyone who says to Me, 'Lord, Lord,' shall enter the kingdom of heaven, but he who does the*

will of My Father in heaven. Many will say to Me in that day, 'Lord, Lord, have we not prophesied in Your name, cast out demons in Your name, and done many wonders in Your name?' And then I will declare to them, 'I never knew you; depart from Me, you who practice lawlessness!'"

I believe (this is my personal opinion) that the reason Jesus did not know them, is because they were not doing any of those things in love. Instead, they were doing them for monetary gain, personal recognition, or perhaps even to gain favor with God or get into heaven. They didn't have relationship with him and so they didn't have God's love flowing through them. We can be doing all the right things, but if we aren't doing them in love, then Jesus will not recognize them or us.

A true disciple will first, have a deep and intimate love relationship with God through daily meditation in His Word and in prayer. Out of that love relationship with God will come the love for others that will cause believers and non-believers to recognize you as a true disciple of Jesus Christ!

Discussion for Chapter 12: Loving

1. Discuss the biblical definition of love and how that is different from worldly love.

2. Jesus said that they (non-believers) would know we were his disciples by our love for one another. What does that look like to you?

3. Looking at the love described in 1 Corinthians 13, how are you doing with loving your spouse, kids, boss, neighbors, pastor, those who attend your church?

4. How is it possible that we could love the way the chapter described or even love our enemies?

CHAPTER THIRTEEN

†

GIVING

Growing up, I never really saw external generosity modeled. My dad worked and mom stayed home, so we didn't lack, but there wasn't much extra money. Christmas was always a time when we experienced internal generosity, as there were plenty of gifts and at times some very expensive items. Receiving gifts was fun for me and I could tell my parents enjoyed giving the gifts.

As a child, Christmas was mostly about the tree, decorating, carols, Santa, and presents under the tree. As I mentioned previously, we went to church and I knew that Christmas was about Jesus too. I just didn't grasp the importance of the greatest gift ever given.

> *"For God so loved the world that he gave his one and only Son, that whoever believes in him shall not perish but have eternal life."* [John 3:16]

In the last chapter, we talked about love and here we see that it was out of God's love that He gave His only Son to be a one-time sacrifice to redeem our sins and bring us back into right relationship (righteousness) with God.

God is the original giver. He gave us a perfect world and when we messed it up, He gave us a sacrificial system, and when we messed that up, He gave us His Son as the ultimate sacrifice. One day soon, God will give us (true believers/disciples) that perfect world back and we will spend eternity with Him in heaven on earth.

Genesis 1:26 says that God made man in God's image and likeness. Part of that likeness is the giving nature. Deep down inside, everyone likes to give. Even those who are not believers in Jesus like to give. Unfortunately, the sin nature that lives inside all of us is greedy and doesn't like to give. That's why there is often a tug-of-war when we want to be generous, particularly if it's going to be a sacrifice of our time or money.

Typically, when we talk about giving, it's regarding money, but in this chapter, we're going to look at three types of giving that Jesus expects of his true disciples – money, time, and talents. The scriptures are filled with teaching and wisdom on all three, so let's get started.

Money

This is always the touchiest of all the giving topics, so let's tackle it first. Money is a major stronghold in the lives of many Christians. They say that they've given themselves totally to God, except in the area of money. Oh, they are at the church every time the door is open and they even volunteer when people are needed, but they put a $20 bill in the offering plate each week and call it good. I've spoken with people who've said, "God doesn't need my money, He walks on streets of gold, the church will just misuse the money, and I need the money more than God or the church does."

Out of complete transparency, I must admit I was one of those. I figured if God was that rich, He certainly didn't need my little bit of money and the big church I was attending wouldn't miss it. The interesting fact was that I wasn't good with money until I started practicing the biblical principles of giving. More on that later.

Many Christians are even tired of (and even get offended at) pastors talking about money, but it appears that the Bible talks about money more than any other single topic. The way I look at it is that if the Bible talks about something once, it's important and if it talks about something twenty times, it must be extremely important. The word *money* shows up 125 times in the King James Version, 134 times in the New American Standard Bible, 113 times in the New International Version, and 197 times in the New Living Translation. So, what does it say about money that the Bible talks about it at least 113 times? I would say that God thinks it's an important topic and He wants us to have His wisdom when it comes to money. So, let's look at a few of these scriptures about money.

Let's go right to the one we hear the most, although it's usually misquoted.

> *"For the love of money is a root of all kinds of evil. Some people, eager for money, have wandered from the faith and pierced themselves with many griefs."* [1 Timothy 6:10]

Most people think that it says that money is the root of all evil, but that's the influence of satan. He doesn't want Christians to have money, as they are more likely to do good things with it. On the flip side, God doesn't want His children to love money more than Him. In fact, Matthew 6:24 says that money can be a master and that we can't serve both God and money.

The key to not making money our master or god, is to let God lead us to give it to people in need. We, the true disciples, are supposed to be rivers not reservoirs. God wants to get the money to us so we can give it to those in need. We aren't to hoard money. Instead of building up a stockpile of treasure here on earth (that we can't take with us when we die), we are to build up treasure in heaven by helping people with the money God gives us. Here are some scriptures that talk about the ill effects of trusting in money, instead of God:

> *"Such are the paths of all who go after ill-gotten gain; it takes away the life of those who get it."*
> [Proverbs 1:19]

> *"Those who trust in their riches will fall..."*
> [Proverbs 11:28]

> *"Whoever loves money never has enough; whoever loves wealth is never satisfied with their income."* [Ecclesiastes 5:10]

It's clear that God wants to protect His children from the damaging effects of money. Think about it this way. Would you give a $100 bill to a baby? Of course not, it would go right in the mouth, because the baby has no way of knowing the value. A teenager with a $100 bill knows the value, but will probably misspend it, because they haven't been taught the principles of handling money. Now, an adult, who has been taught biblical financial principles, will tithe $10, probably give another $10, save $10, and then use the rest to pay bills or do things with the family.

The answer isn't to not have any money, because you can't help the poor if you are one. As true disciples, we are to recognize that money is just a tool and it really doesn't belong to you, because everything belongs to God (Psalm 24:1, 1 Corinthians 10:26, Hebrews 2:10). We don't own money, we are just stewarding the money God gives us. So, let's look at how we are to handle money.

1. Be faithful with what you have – I speak and write a lot on money and often people will tell me that when God blesses them with a bunch of money, they will give big (actually, it's usually when they win the lottery, they will give big). The fact is, if someone isn't a giver with a little, they probably won't be a giver when they have a lot. Plus, God rewards those who are faithful with little. We see that in the parable of the talents (Matthew 25:14-30) and minas (Luke 19:11-27). The master, who represents Jesus, told the two faithful servants who invested wisely, that they had been faithful with little so he would now entrust them with much. When you are faithful with what you have, God can trust you with more. However, He will never give you more money than you can handle, so if you don't have much money, take a close look at your giving records. Perhaps you need to start giving more and ask God for wisdom on how to better handle the money He is giving you now.

2. Be content with what you have – I find so many people who have a home, job, family, clothes, food, water, good health, a running car, and so much more and yet they are never happy. Did you know that if your household income is more than $32,400 annually, you are in the top 1% of income earners worldwide?[1] In Philippians 4, Paul talks about how he has become content whether he has a lot or a little. That's trusting in God and being content with what He gives you. Now, you can certainly ask Him for more or for the wisdom to increase your wealth and if you have shown yourself faithful, He may promote you or show you a way to earn more.

3. Remember it's not your money – As I showed you earlier, everything belongs to God, so you never have any money that is yours. Rather, God has entrusted His money to you to use correctly by taking care of your needs (not all those crazy wants) and then being a blessing to others with the rest. He doesn't even mind if you splurge on occasion. Maintain the heart of a giver and you'll be fine. So, since it's not your money, hold it loosely and be an obedient servant when God says to give.

4. Tithe – God owns all your money and allows you to partner in the money business. All He asks is that you give Him the first 10% of your increase – that's your paycheck, bonuses, and financial gifts. That 10% belongs to God and if you are not bringing it to the storehouse (church), you are stealing from God. I'm going to talk more about this a little later, so we'll leave it at that.

5. Offerings – Beyond the first 10% (tithe), the Bible says you are to give offerings. The tithe goes to wherever you attend services with the body of Christ. Offerings can be given to anyone who needs help. This includes the church, other ministries, food and clothing banks, homeless shelters, missionaries, and anyone you encounter who is in need. I will also talk more about this later.

6. Trust God as your source – Your job or business is not your source or provider, God is. He may use a job or business or investment portfolio, but ultimately, He is your provider. If you are tithing and giving, you will never lack the basics of life. Jesus taught his disciples to stop worrying about money because God takes care of the birds and flowers and He values mankind much more (Matthew 6:25-33). If we are continually seeking God, He will provide all we need, just as He did with the Israelites in the wilderness.

I mentioned earlier that I was never a very good money manager. It wasn't something that was taught in school, nor did my parents teach me. Consequently, I made a lot of mistakes, particularly when it came to credit. I had to declare bankruptcy in 1986 and by 2000 was $120,000 in debt (not counting our mortgage).

The defining moment was when we (Karen and I) gave up trying to figure it out ourselves and started seeking God for wisdom. The first instruction was to tithe. Well, we thought we couldn't afford to tithe. We were already living on credit cards, doing the old "borrow from Peter to pay Paul approach", because there wasn't enough money to pay the bills.

We fought it for months, but everywhere we went, God would have people teach about tithing. Clearly God wanted us to trust Him, so we finally gave in. When we got paid, we wrote the first check (10% of our gross income) to God and then trusted Him for the rest. An amazing thing happened. We got to the end of the first month and not only did we have enough money to pay the bills, but there was money left over. It didn't make any sense and we couldn't figure it out. We eventually stopped trying and accepted the fact that God's ways are higher than our ways.

Our faith was raised by the tithing experience and my spiritual mentor encouraged us to give 10% beyond the tithe. Similar to what we experienced with tithing, we fought this idea, because there wasn't that much left after paying the tithe and bills. After some time, we once again decided to trust God and began giving 10% above the 10% tithe. We tithed, gave, paid the bills and there was money left over. God is an amazing provider. Do you trust Him?

Once we had a good financial foundation, God began giving us wisdom for getting rid of the debt. We started by eliminating all non-essential expenses – coffee drinks and sodas, meals out, entertainment, cable tv, and such. We were actually surprised at how much we had been spending on these. The extra money was used to pay down the credit card and loan debt.

Next, God told us to sell our family home. We really fought Him on that one, as it was a perfect house for our family and we still had three of our five children at home.

We had lived in our home for ten years and loved it. We had so many memories of our children jumping on the trampoline in the back yard, family movie nights in the basement with hot buttered popcorn in grease stained paper bags, our two grandchildren pulling the dishes out from under the microwave stand, many birthday parties in the dining room, and Christmases in the living room. It was a fantastic family home and we were sad to have to move. However, again, we were obedient, and God blessed us with a rental house that was brand new and the overall monthly cost was much less, which gave us more extra money to put toward paying down debt.

We also downgraded our cars – traded them in on lesser models that would reduce our monthly auto cost. This was a really tough one, because it was when I had to give up the metallic green T-top Camaro. We traded it in on that Honda Civic that was stolen and returned. It's humbling to go from a tricked-out Camaro to a Honda Civic. We also had a fantastic van that fit our entire family. Back then, it was hard to find vehicles that would seat seven. We traded it in on a late model, low mile sedan. These were difficult decisions that had to be made. Again, we applied the difference to debt elimination.

Finally, God gave us a plan to rapidly pay off the credit cards and loans. He had us make a list of all the credit card and loan balances from lowest to highest. We started with the lowest balance card and put all the extra money toward it, until it was paid off. We then cut up the card and closed the account. Then we took that entire payment and added it to what we were paying on the next lowest balance card, until it was paid off. We repeated the process until they were all paid off. I must say, this was an exhilarating experience, as we could watch the balances quickly decrease and disappear. The further we got into the process, the quicker our debt elimination accelerated.

Any time we had extra money – bonuses, commissions,

home business income – we would apply it to the debt reduction plan. Many people had told us to declare bankruptcy; that it would take twenty years or more to pay off the debt. By using God's wise counsel, we were completely debt free within five years. Praise God!

Now, since I know that I struggled with tithing and so many others do, let's take a closer look at the subject. Many people think that tithing was part of the law, that was superseded by grace and that we are no longer required to tithe. Actually, the tithe existed before the law, as we see in Genesis 14:18-20, when Abram tithed to the high priest, Melchizedek:

> *"Then Melchizedek king of Salem brought out bread and wine. He was priest of God Most High, and he blessed Abram, saying, 'Blessed be Abram by God Most High, Creator of heaven and earth. And praise be to God Most High, who delivered your enemies into your hand.' Then Abram gave him a **tenth** of everything."* (emphasis mine)

This person named Melchizedek is interesting. In Genesis 14, he is referred to as the king of Salem and a priest of the God Most High. He shows up again in Hebrews 7. Here we learn that the name Melchizedek means "king of righteousness" and king of Salem means "king of peace". Sound like anyone you know? It goes on to say that he was without father or mother, without genealogy, without beginning of days or end of life, resembling the Son of God, and that he remains a priest forever. Later, Jesus is compared as a priest to Melchizedek, rather than the Levites (Levitical priesthood established by God through Moses).

No one knows who Melchizedek was, but some biblical scholars believe he was the Son of God, who appeared momentarily in human form (as the angels did quite often

149

throughout the Bible). In any case, Abram recognized divinity and gave him a tithe of the spoils of his conquest.

If we jump forward to the time after the cross, we, like Abram/Abraham, recognize divinity and bring our tithe (which means 10%) to Jesus. We may put it in a plate, bucket, basket, or bag during a church service or pay it online or by texting, but in the spiritual realm we are giving God back His share.

Back to the argument that the tithe is part of the law and so we no longer are required to tithe. This is true, but if they were required to tithe under the law (which was actually about 23.3%[2]), how much more should we give under grace? 10% should be the minimum we give. Jesus gave it all! He's just asking for 10% back and offering some great promises in return (see Malachi 3:8-12). That seems like a great deal to me, how about you?

In Genesis 28:22, we see Jacob (later renamed Israel), the father of the 12 tribes, making a vow to God to give Him a tenth. Earlier, we saw his father, Abraham, giving a tithe and now Jacob offers to give a tithe. How did they know to do this? Clearly, before the law was created, God had talked with His people about tithing (giving 10% of what He blessed them with). Later, man added this to the law. Jesus said he didn't come to abolish the law, but to fulfill it.

Jesus himself confirmed the tithe in Matthew 23:23 and Luke 11:42, when he told the teachers of the law and Pharisees that they should continue practicing the tithe, but should also not neglect justice, mercy, and faithfulness. Certainly, if we were not supposed to tithe, Jesus would not have said this.

Granted, we don't see any other references to tithing in the New Testament, but Paul does mention something that sounds a lot like a tithe in 1 Corinthians 16:2:

"On the first day of every week, each one of you

should set aside a sum of money in keeping with your income, saving it up, so that when I come no collections will have to be made."

Now, neither tithe nor 10% is mentioned, so it's possible that it was the grace version of tithing or that these people already knew about tithing. We don't know for sure, but in any case, under grace, we should be giving at least 10% and as much as we can; as the more we give, the more God feels comfortable with our handling of money and can bless us more.

Time and Talents

God doesn't just want us to give money. He has also given us time and talents that we can contribute to the body of Christ. We see this throughout the entire Bible:

- Noah was a carpenter, so God had him build the ark that saved mankind.
- Joseph was a problem solver, who could interpret dreams and God used him to save Israel and his twelve sons.
- Moses was trained in leadership while living in Egypt, so God used him to lead the Israelites out of captivity.
- Bezalel and Oholiab were gifted craftsmen who used their talents to construct and furnish the tabernacle of God.
- Peter had the gift of gab and so God used him to give the first sermon, from which 3,000 were saved.
- Paul was a talented writer and expert in the scriptures, so God used him to write a large portion of the New Testament.

God gives us talents, that He will use through us, to

further the Kingdom on earth. What are your talents and how can God use them?

Although I was an introverted kid, I discovered that I had a talent for leadership early in life. I was the one organizing the tag, baseball, basketball, and football games. I organized the kids into teams to build a neighborhood fort. In elementary school, I was voted the student council president and in High School was a captain of the varsity baseball team. In college I was voted in as the secretary of my fraternity.

After graduating from college I quickly rose from the ranks into corporate management and then launched my own businesses. Within two years of being saved, I was launching and leading a men's ministry at a church of over 2,000 and later was asked to lead the volunteer effort for two large Promise Keeper events. God called me to be a pastor and I led two churches and a ministry.

All that said, God has a way of keeping leaders humble. Paul had his thorn (2 Corinthians 12:7) and I had many thorns. At age twelve I was cut from an elite baseball team too late to play for another team. I had to play in a city league with no uniforms.

It was humbling, but it was also a growing experience. As a business owner, I had several failed businesses and neither of the churches I helped plant are still around (they are both long stories that aren't relevant to this book). I mentioned earlier a failed marriage, bankruptcy and so on. I've always said that failures are the steppingstones to success, but they definitely keep a leader humble.

What about you? Can you look back through your life and see how you always seemed to be in a leadership role? If so, then that's a talent God has given you to serve the body of Christ.

God also gave me the ability to write. Again, I discovered this early in my life, when I found out other kids struggled with writing projects and I excelled. Now, don't ask me to solve a math problem or talk about history or science, as I have no talent in those areas. In high school, my creative writing teacher told me I could be a great writer someday. That comment had a huge impact on my life. During college I earned extra money by helping people write their term papers and was a writer for the school newspaper. In the business world, I used this talent to write powerful proposals and business plans, copy for marketing materials and advertising, newspaper and newsletter articles. I also published several business and Christian books. In ministry I've written 501(c)3 applications, ministry plans, books, articles, and blogs. Just a quick warning, being gifted doesn't mean everything will go well. Several of my books never sold well and I have two that are still unpublished.

What Are Your Gifts?

Are you gifted at writing? Perhaps there is a life changing book inside you or you could help someone else write their book. Maybe your church needs someone to write social media and blog posts. Perhaps there are ministries and non-profits in your community who could use a talented writer.

As I said earlier, I was a shy kid, so speaking was not my thing. One of my favorite television programs is America's Got Talent and I'm always amazed at the poise of the young people who sing, dance, do acrobatics, and tell jokes. When I was young, I would have rather died than stand in front of a group of people to do anything. In fact, in college I negotiated with my advisor to get out of some speech classes. I did, however, take debate and found that I was good at arguing (of course I already knew that). My Mom always told me I should be a lawyer, because I was good at arguing; or a doctor, because no one could read my handwriting. I found out there was more to the life of a lawyer than just arguing and more to being a doctor than scratchy handwriting, and so I pursued neither.

In my first six years after college, I was involved in sales, which required one-on-one and small group presentations. I was very comfortable in those settings. After launching my first business, I realized that to get ahead, I needed to be a good public speaker, so I forced myself into speaking engagements. The first one was so bad that I sweat through two shirts and a suit jacket before I said a word and then, with sweat pouring down my forehead, I read the entire speech and barely looked up. My second speech was worse, as my mouth dried up so bad that my tongue stuck to the roof of my mouth. That was massively embarrassing, but I was determined to conquer the fear. From that point on, each speech was better. Now I love getting up in front of a group and have spoken to groups of over 5,000.

God has used this talent for speaking to deliver powerful sermons and teach life changing information through me. He's used it to guide people to Jesus, help them get out of debt, and save marriages. How about you? Do you have that gift of gab? If not, can you work through the fear and let God use you to impact people's lives through speaking? You might teach children or adult classes at your church, give seminars that could positively impact the body of Christ, or preach the gospel at a rescue mission or homeless shelter or prison.

Maybe you have talents in building or fixing things. God could use you on a mission trip to help build homes or churches. Perhaps you could help fix or remodel a home for a senior shut-in, or single Mom. You could join forces with a non-profit organization that builds or remodels homes for low-income families.

Are you talented artistically? You could help churches and ministries with logos, drawings for visual aids or promotional materials, or perhaps graphic design for brochures, PowerPoint presentations, and training guides.

Can you sing or play an instrument? Maybe God wants you to consider being on the worship team or writing worship songs. You could go, with a small group, to an area where the homeless live and share your gift of music while the group passes out water and sandwiches. You could go to a park and attract people with your music, creating an opportunity for you or others to minister the gospel.

Are you highly organized and good with numbers? Every church and ministry need someone to handle the books and financial recordkeeping. You might also help with the office work and become a huge blessing to the church or ministry.

Do you find technology easy and fascinating? That's fantastic! Churches and ministries need people to help with sound, recording, build websites, set up online and text giving, and more. These technology talents are extremely valuable for the good of the Kingdom!

Once you've recognized your talents, the next step is to consult with your spiritual leaders on how best to use your talents.

Proverbs 15:22 (NASB) says, *"Without consultation, plans are frustrated, but with many counselors they succeed."* These counselors should be mature Christians, church leaders, pastors, Christian parents or friends. While you are consulting with others, continue praying about God's plans for using the talents He gave you. Ask Him how and where you might serve. Once you have some direction, get into action using your talents for the good of the Kingdom.

As true disciples, God wants us to give of our time, talents, and money. Nothing belongs to us. We were bought with a price – the steepest price of all time – and so we and everything in our lives belong to God.

END NOTES

1. https://www.investopedia.com/articles/personal-finance/050615/are-you-top-one-percent-world.asp
2. https://www.generouschurch.com/tithing-questions

Discussion for Chapter 13: Giving

1. With all honesty, how does it make you feel, when a pastor, preacher, evangelist or anyone else starts talking about money?

2. Are you tithing? If so, share how that has changed your life. If not, why not?

3. Describe some ways you have given of your time and/or talent.

4. How could you improve your giving of money, time, and talents?

CHAPTER FOURTEEN

†

INVADING

Before I became a Christian, I believed in re-incarnation. I thought for sure that I was a military general in some past life. Why did I think that? Good question, I'm glad you asked. In almost every part of my life, I was very strategic. I know it's not popular now, but as a kid, I loved playing war and I was always the one drawing up the battle plans. Later, we played capture the flag and tag, where I used strategy to win nearly every time. I carried strategy into football and was the guy making up the plays. I also learned the game of chess early and was very good at it. My favorite board games Risk and Feudal, required strategy and not just luck. In the business world, I continued to use strategy to become the top salesperson or build successful businesses. When God called me to help plant a church, I used strategy to help the church grow.

The really cool thing is that God is a strategist too. He used strategy to create a perfect universe and place the earth in just the right place, so that human life could abound. He used strategy, after the fall of man, to redeem sin through animal sacrifices. It was His strategy that placed Jesus on the earth at the perfect time and it will be His strategy that brings Jesus back to earth as a conquering King.

If you haven't recognized it by now, we are in a war. There is an enemy named satan, who hates God and all His children. His mission in life is to steal, kill, and destroy (John 10:10). All Christians are his targets. We are literally running around with a target on our backs (and fronts).

> *"And from the time John the Baptist began preaching until now, the Kingdom of Heaven has been forcefully advancing, and violent people are attacking it."* [Matthew 11:12 NLT] (emphasis mine)

The Kingdom of God is invading earth and we are the invasion force! We can see this in Genesis 1:27-28:

> *"So God created mankind in his own image, in the image of God he created them; male and female he created them. God blessed them and said to them, 'Be fruitful and increase in number; fill the earth and subdue it. Rule over the fish in the sea and the birds in the sky and over every living creature that moves on the ground.'"* (emphasis mine)

The Hebrew word that is translated as "subdue" is kabash, which means to force, bring into bondage, make subservient, dominate, and tread down. Creator God is giving Adam and Eve a commandment to forcefully take over the rest of the earth. Why would that be, when they were living in a beautiful paradise? Because God only created paradise (Eden) in one geographic location. The rest of the earth needed transformation and since Lucifer and one-third of the angels had been cast to the earth, due to their rebellion against God, there would be a constant battle to spread Eden throughout the rest of the planet.

Unlike the Civil War, World Wars, Korean War, Vietnam War, Gulf War and others in the middle east, we are not warring against other people. The following scripture makes this clear and also reveals who we are fighting against in our everyday life.

> *"For our struggle is not against flesh and blood, but against the rulers, against the authorities, against the powers of this dark world and against the spiritual forces of evil in the heavenly realms."* [Ephesians 6:12]

We don't fight against people, we fight against satan and his demonic hoard. Now, this can freak some people out, because we can't see the devil and demons, so how can we fight them. The good news is found in Ephesians 6:13-17:

> *"Therefore put on the full armor of God, so that when the day of evil comes, you may be able to stand your ground, and after you have done everything, to stand. Stand firm then, with the belt of truth buckled around your waist, with the breastplate of righteousness in place, and with your feet fitted with the readiness that comes from the gospel of peace. In addition to all this, take up the shield of faith, with which you can extinguish all the flaming arrows of the evil one. Take the helmet of salvation and the sword of the Spirit, which is the word of God."*

Our job is to put on the full armor of God to protect us from the enemy attacks. We are to use the shield of faith to ward off the flaming arrows of the enemy. We are to stand still, stay in peace, and let God and the other two-thirds of the angels fight the battles for us.

As we saw in the chapter on authority, satan has no power over us, except when we give it. He can attack all he wants, but it's just words (lies). I find it interesting that in 1 Peter 5:8, the devil is described as a roaring lion, prowling around seeking someone to devour. Unfortunately, we often misinterpret this scripture and give the devil more power than he really deserves. If you study lions, you will find that a roaring lion is not a hungry lion, it's the quiet ones you should worry about. So, satan is roaring, but his roar has no power – it's just a bunch of noise. It also says that he's seeking someone to devour, not that he's devouring people. He speaks lies (Jesus called him the father of lies) and waits to see if people accept those lies and if so, then he can begin to devour them.

For this reason, the apostle Paul taught in 2 Corinthians 10:5:

"We demolish arguments and every pretension that sets itself up against the knowledge of God, and we take captive every thought to make it obedient to Christ."

In the garden, when Lucifer (the serpent) spoke to Eve, he used speculations and lofty things that were against what God told Adam. If Adam and Eve had taken those thoughts captive and asked God about them, we would all be living in Eden with God.

When satan and his demonic army comes at you with speculations and lofty things, you need to be able to recognize them. So, the first step in this is to know the Word of God. When the devil tried to tempt Jesus in the wilderness, with his speculations and lofty things, Jesus responded each time with, "it is written" and quoted him scripture. If you don't know the Word of God (internalized and memorized), you won't be able to recognize and respond to satan's deception by saying, "It is written . . ."

Given what we've been talking about, the title of the chapter, *Invading*, might seem strange, but it's God's original intention for mankind. Inadvertently, the church has been in defense mode for over 2,000 years. However, as we saw from Genesis 1:28, we were to invade and subdue the earth, which is the opposite of the defensive stance the church has taken. God still expects us to subdue the earth and the only way we can do that is to lead a heavenly invasion.

God's intention for Adam and Eve was for them to multiply the number of perfect human beings, who would all walk in God's sinless glory, making more perfect human beings who would fill the earth with God's glory. As born-again believers and true disciples of Jesus Christ, our mission is similar. We are first to be fruitful and multiply. In other words, we are to preach the gospel to everyone and make new disciples. Second, we are to equip those disciples, so that they can also be fruitful and multiply. Finally, we are to violently subdue the sinful earth, with the authority Jesus gave to all believers. We accomplish this through prayer.

In Matthew 16:19 we see that Jesus gave us the keys of the Kingdom of heaven and that whatever we bind (forbid) on earth shall be bound in heaven. Jesus also said, in Mark 3:27, the only way to overpower the strong man (referring to satan), is for someone stronger to bind him. We aren't strong enough to do that, so we must turn to someone stronger; that would be Jesus. There is power in the name of Jesus and in the spoken Word, which enables us to bind demons, when we encounter them. We bind them through our words and then God, through His angels, will stop that demonic activity in heaven. Remember that we don't fight against flesh and blood. When people are engaged in repetitive willful sin, such as addictions or even anger, most of the time they are motivated by a demonic entity. If we bind that activity, it will usually stop. If not, then it's just them operating in the flesh.

Angels

Although Lucifer deceived one third of the angels and led them in rebellion against God, there are still twice that many angels who are loyal to God and His mission with mankind on the earth. God's angels are important to our mission to invade the world and in the war against satan and the fallen angels, as they are the only beings that can battle in the heavenly realm. We can't see satan and the demons, so it's impossible for us to fight them. We must rely on God and His angels to fight for us.

Now, there has been a lot of controversy about angels. Some people focus too much attention on them and can even get into angel worship. They are created beings, like we are. We are to worship God only. The angels are there to help God's children (Hebrews 1:14), so we also shouldn't ignore them. As I said earlier, they are important in the strategy to win the daily battles, as we invade the world with the gospel of Jesus Christ and make earth look more like heaven.

Our words are important in the battles, as we have been given the ability to loose (permit or release) things on earth that will be loosed in heaven. First, we can loose God's angels to battle for us. Psalm 91:9-11 reads:

> "If you make the Lord your refuge, if you make the Most High your shelter, no evil will conquer you; no plague will come near your home. For He will order His angels to protect you wherever you go." (emphasis mine)

I love the story in 2 Kings 6:8-23, when the King of Aram sent an army to kill the prophet Elisha, because God kept telling him where and when the Arameans were going to attack. In the middle of the night the army had Elisha surrounded and his servant awoke to see the enemy army. Elisha told him not to be afraid and prayed that God would open the servant's eyes to see into the spirit realm. When God did, the servant could see that the hillside was covered with angels on horses and in chariots of fire.

There are many stories of angels protecting missionaries in foreign countries. One that comes to mind is the one told by John G. Paton, a missionary to the New Hebrides Islands. He told how hostile natives surrounded their mission headquarters and were planning to burn the building with them in it. They prayed all night and the attackers finally left. A year later, the chief of the tribe was converted to Christianity and when Paton asked him about that night, the chief said that hundreds of big men in shining garments with drawn swords surrounded the building, so the natives were afraid to attack. Paton confirmed that there were no human soldiers anywhere near and that must have been angels answering their prayers[1].

Angel Encounter

I have a friend who was attending a church in a rough part of town. One night they were praying for the area late into the night and as he was leaving the church building, he prayed that the Lord would protect him. Walking toward his car, three large gang bangers stepped between my friend and his car. It was easy to see that they had ill intent in mind. My friend thanked Jesus for protection and suddenly the leader's eyes moved to behind and above my friend. Wide eyed and terrified, the leader stumbled backwards, running into the other two gang members, who also looked terrified. All three turned and ran away. Now, my friend is not a big man, but he had several large Samoan friends who were at the church. When he turned, expecting to see some of his friends, no one was there. He was convinced that at least one mighty angel had appeared momentarily, and my friend was protected.

Psalm 103:20 says that angels obey the voice of God's Word. Jesus gave us authority to speak the Word in power. Hebrews 1:14 tells us that angels are sent to serve for the sake of those who are to inherit salvation. That's us (believers).

Angels will also bring answers to our prayers, as we see in Daniel 10. The story begins in Daniel 9 when Daniel is praying for his people. He was confessing his own sin and the sins of the people and pleading with the Lord for Jerusalem. Gabriel, the messenger angel appears to Daniel and gives him a prophetic word about the future (Daniel 9:20-27). Then in Daniel 10 an angel appears to him and tells him that God answered his prayer the moment it was spoken, but for twenty-one days, this angel had fought with the spirit prince of the kingdom of Persia (a demonic principality) and that the archangel Michael had to come fight to free him to deliver the answer to Daniel.

The key here is that we don't pray to angels and we don't ask angels to do things. We pray to Father God, in the name of Jesus, and He will dispatch the angels to protect and battle for us. Personally, I've never seen an angel, but I have sensed when both demons and angels are around. I also know that angels have protected me at times. So, as a part of our battle plan, as we continue to invade and subdue the earth, angels will play an important part.

Finances

Another key to invading is finances. It costs money to take the gospel to the world, so we also need to loose funds for the invasion. It's exciting to know that Father God has unlimited wealth and He will release the funds necessary. Now, before you freak out and close the book, I'm not talking about some name it, claim it teaching, where we treat God like Santa Clause or some cosmic genie. No, what I'm talking about is a form of spiritual warfare that relates to the previous thoughts about angels.

Our loving heavenly Father knows that we need money to live and spread the gospel. Through Jesus, He told the disciples not to worry about where they would get money to live the everyday life (Matthew 6:25-34). Jesus said that if his Father took care of the birds and flowers, why wouldn't He take care of His children. So, we just need to remain in faith that God will take care of us and not let worry creep in. That said, you can't sit around your house watching TV or playing video games and expect God to provide. He does expect us to work.

With Vision There is Provision

Something else that I've discovered is that when God gives someone a vision for a church, ministry, business or invention, there will also be an attached provision. In other words, when God gives the idea, He also provides the funds to make the idea a reality.

When we planted our first church in 2001, it was a clear vision from God, and He provided abundant provision. Unlike most small churches, we had more money than we needed. Every Monday we would gather our finance team and pray about what to do with the extra funds. First, we would check with the congregation to see if there were any needs and fill those. With what remained, we would find a church that was expanding and sow financial seed into their building project. At times, we gave to ministries that helped feed, clothe, or house the poor.

One of my favorite projects was when our small church body raised and delivered $12,000 to help another church remodel an old ice-skating rink. The building was about two hours away and we also brought a team of our guys to help with the remodel. The remodeling allowed for expansion of that church and more of the earth subdued.

Now, whether it's money for your personal needs or a new venture, God doesn't just rain down money or plant a money tree in the backyard or have money just appear (well actually money appearing out of nowhere has happened to a few people). More often the money will come from natural sources, but it will come supernaturally.

As I mentioned earlier, prior to gaining knowledge about God's financial system, Karen and I had many financial struggles. Since gaining Biblical wisdom on finances, we've never struggled. That doesn't mean we haven't had faith challenging times. In fact, between 2012 and 2016, we were often walking in faith, as a long-time business failed, and we lost our income.

Supernatural Funds

A great example of needed funds coming supernaturally through a natural source was when we needed $400 to pay a bill and it was due in a couple days. I went to the mailbox and there was a check for a little more than $400 from an internet business that hadn't produced a check of more than $30 in several years and hasn't since. God knew we needed that money, so He produced it supernaturally through a natural source. This has happened many times in many ways.

At the end of the economic downturn (2008 to 2011), we encountered a very challenging situation. After our business failed, I spent over a year job hunting. The market was very competitive and unemployment numbers were high. Eventually, I secured a job in business development. I had extreme favor at the job. In just seven months I made enough to pay the bills and bank $12,000.

During that time, we had also been led by the Lord to a new church, where I also had extreme favor. The pastor at this new church was interested in hiring me to be the executive pastor and we set a start day. I gave notice at my job and helped them hire and train my replacement. The week I was supposed to start the pastor job, some things came up and then the funding was not available, so I was once again unemployed.

We had thought the $12,000 was savings for our future, but God knew all of this was going to happen, so He gave us the necessary money in advance. At the writing of this book, I'm back with the same company, doing business development. This time, my starting salary was $10,000 per year higher and I've received another $10,000 per year raise. I've continued to have extreme favor and we were able to replace the savings previously used.

The Key is Prayer

The key to these stories is prayer. It's first losing the money and second destroying the spiritual blockades that satan and his demonic army will set up to keep the funds from reaching you. Just like Daniel, we must keep praying, so that God's angels can fight through the demonic forces to bring the answer. Since we have authority over satan and his demons, all we do is pray and God's angels go to work for us. I'm sure Daniel was probably expecting a quicker answer and it took 21 days. Sometimes the answer will come quickly and sometimes it takes time. That's where faith and the spiritual fruit of patience (or long-suffering) comes in.

Worship

Worship is also an important part of our invasion battle strategy, as it changes the atmosphere to be more like heaven. There have been so many times, when I've been under heavy stress, feeling like the world was pressing in on me from every direction (can you relate?) and I would start playing some worship music and all that pressure would fade away. I've noticed it at church services too. People would be busily rushing around and there was a tense atmosphere. Then worship begins and the peace of God settles on the sanctuary.

There are a number of Bible stories where worship was a key battle strategy. Let's take a look at my favorite worship in battle story:

> *"Early in the morning they left for the Desert of Tekoa. As they set out, Jehoshaphat stood and said, 'Listen to me, Judah and people of Jerusalem! Have faith in the LORD your God and you will be upheld; have faith in his prophets and you will be successful.' After consulting the people, Jehoshaphat appointed men to sing to the LORD and to praise him for the splendor of his holiness as they went out at the head of the army, saying: 'Give thanks to the LORD, for his love endures forever.' As they began to sing and praise, the LORD set ambushes against the men of Ammon and Moab and Mount Seir who were invading Judah, and they were defeated."*
> [2 Chronicles 20:21-22]

As you can see in this story, God had given King Jehoshaphat a unique battle plan. He was to send out worshippers before the army, and as they worshipped, God set ambushes that defeated the enemies. It appears that King Jehoshaphat's army didn't even have to fight.

Another great worship during battle story is found in the book of Joshua, when the Israelites were faced with the fortified city of Jericho. Let's take a look at God's plan for defeating this highly fortified city:

"Now the gates of Jericho were securely barred because of the Israelites. No one went out and no one came in. Then the LORD said to Joshua, 'See, I have delivered Jericho into your hands, along with its king and its fighting men. March around the city once with all the armed men. Do this for six days. Have seven priests carry trumpets of rams' horns in front of the ark. On the seventh day, march around the city seven times, with the priests blowing the trumpets. When you hear them sound a long blast on the trumpets, have the whole army give a loud shout; then the wall of the city will collapse and the army will go up, everyone straight in.'" [Joshua 6:1-5]

Have you ever put yourself in Joshua's shoes? He has millions of Israelites following him into the promised land. They are now facing a massive fortified city, and this is the plan God gives Joshua. I wonder what Joshua was thinking or how his generals responded, when he shared God's unique plan. I can hear them now, "So, let me get this straight, we're going to send seven priests out blowing trumpets and we're going to walk around the city once a day for six days and then seven times on the seventh day. Then we're going to all shout and the walls will fall down. Joshua, are you positive that was God?"

Knowing human nature, I'm sure there was some doubt and yet they were obedient, and it happened exactly as God said it would. In fact, when you study the Hebrew, it indicates that the rubble from the walls went down into the earth and the Israelite army walked into Jericho on flat ground.

Blowing the trumpets was worship and prepared the atmosphere for God's creative miracle of disappearing walls. Worship will do the same in your daily battles. It confuses the enemy, changes the atmosphere, and opens your situation up for creative miracles. So, your battle plan should include starting your day with worship - worship in the car, listening to worship at your workplace (if it's allowed), and having worship music playing at home. When you are facing difficult situations or decisions, set aside time to have a dedicated worship time. Worship wins battles!

Invading Army

We are an invading army in enemy territory and to wage successful warfare, we will need to loose angels to fight in the spirit realm and money to finance the war. The good news is that our job is purely to pray and listen for the voice of God. Then do whatever He says to do.

Some pastor friends of mine have churches in an area called the "hilltop" in Tacoma, WA. Back in the late 80's and early 90's it was one of the most dangerous areas in the United States, as rival gangs the Crips and Bloods battled it out nightly.

These pastors were grieved from so many funerals for members of their congregation who were caught in the crossfire. Their hearts were heavy seeing children getting hooked on cocaine and crack that was sold openly on the streets, and watching good people have to sell their homes for a loss to move to a safer area.

Most people would have just complained, but they declared war against the spiritual forces of wickedness that were motivating the gang members.

These bold pastors began 24-hour prayer in their churches and walked the area during the day, reclaiming it for Jesus. As the violence decreased and at God's prompting, they started walking the streets at night, talking with the drug dealers and gang members, sharing the gospel and love of Jesus with them. Soon a few were saved, and they began ministering to those they knew. Others were saved and over time, the key gang leaders were either saved or left town. Today, that area of Tacoma, is filled with nice homes and is one of the safest places in Washington state.

If we do our part, God will do His, just like He did in the hilltop story and earlier in the story about Elisha and the Aramean army. He did the same thing for king Jehoshaphat when the armies of the Moabites, Ammonites and Meunites marched against Judah. He instructed all the people to fast and pray and God told them not to be afraid or discouraged, because the battle was not theirs, but God's. God caused the attacking armies to turn on themselves and kill each other.

Mighty Man of Valor

My favorite invading story is in Judges 7. Gideon had an army of 32,000 men and was going to fight the Midianites and Amalekites, but God told him he had too many men, so through a series of events, God whittled Gideon's army down to 300 men. God then told Gideon to divide them into 3 groups of 100. He was to give each man a trumpet and a jar with a torch inside. They were to surround the enemy camp and at the signal, blow the trumpets and shout, *"For the Lord and for Gideon"* and then break the jars. When they did this, God threw the armies (as numerous as locusts), into a confused frenzy and they killed each other. Gideon's army was vastly outnumbered in the natural, but they won the battle and didn't even have to fight, except to hunt down some who fled the camp.

God is more powerful than satan and all his demons combined. He already cast satan out of heaven to earth and Jesus conquered him on the cross. We now have the authority to win the battles and eventually Jesus will come back and win the war once and for all. In the meantime, we need to continue invading the land, spreading the gospel of Jesus and making disciples; who then go spread the gospel and make disciples, who also go and spread the gospel and make disciples, who . . . I think you're getting the picture. We can't have an apathetic attitude that someone else will do it. I can hear some of you right now, "the pastors and evangelists will do all of that, I'm too busy just trying to make it".

We weren't put here on earth to sit around complaining about how bad it's getting; we are to subdue it. We are to take it by spiritual force, through prayer and our testimony. Revelation 12:11 says that true disciples will triumph over satan by *"the blood of the Lamb and by the word of their testimony; they did not love their lives so much as to shrink back from death".*

You Volunteered

When you accepted Jesus as your Savior, you volunteered for heaven's invading army. We were issued heavenly armor (Ephesians 6) – the helmet of salvation, breastplate of righteousness, belt of truth, shoes of peace, shield of faith, and sword of the Spirit (Word of God). Hopefully, you have received sword training; how to use the Word of God in battle (as Jesus did with satan in the wilderness) and if not, it's never too late. Find a pastor who teaches the Bible with power or take some Bible classes through a Christian university. Invest time every day meditating over the Bible and journaling about what you learn and hear from the Lord. Set a goal to memorize a certain number of scriptures each month. This will improve your faith and enable you to confidently go into daily battle.

We also need to know our enemy, satan, and his plans of attack. In 2 Corinthians 2:11, Paul wrote, *"... in order that satan should not outwit us. For we are not unaware of his schemes."* The good news is that he's not creative and has been using the same methods of attack for years.

174

First, as he did with Eve in the Garden of Eden, he will twist God's words to make you question whether God really has your best interests in mind.

Second, he will out and out lie to you about the pleasure of sin and minimize the potential devastating outcomes. Once you sin, he will then condemn you, causing guilt and shame.

Third, he will always attack you in your weak times (when you are tired or have had a bad day at work or a fight with your spouse or are having financial struggles). Satan will also use other people to lead us into sin, distract us from our relationship with God, and deceive us; so, we need to be aware of the motives of people around us. Yes, even other Christians, family members, and friends.

Jesus came to destroy the works of the devil (1 John 3:8). He has passed all His authority to the true disciples and yet, as we see with Jesus, we are not to go out demon hunting, as many misguided Christians have done.

The only demons we see Jesus confront are those in the people he was healing. They came to him. Our job is to do as Jesus did and destroy the works of satan by introducing Christ to everyone we meet, pray for the sick, lovingly take care of those in need, and constantly expand the Kingdom on earth.

Time is short. Jesus could return any day and he is relying on us to subdue the earth, so "ATTENTION!", here is your battle plan:

1. **Meditate over scriptures** – Carve out time every day to read and meditate in the scriptures. Join a Bible study with other believers and study together. Fill your mind and heart with the Word of God, so you are prepared for battle. As we approach the end of this time, there will be many false teachers and prophets arise to deceive. It will be so intense that the Bible says that it's possible even the elect could be deceived. The only way you will ensure your

protection is if you have enough of the Word inside you to recognize the false teachings.

Many years ago, I worked for a company that printed checks for banks. In a training class I learned that tellers are trained to spot counterfeit checks and currency by studying the intricate detail of the real thing, which makes it easy to spot the fake. We must do this as well. Study the real thing – the Bible – so you can recognize the fake.

2. **Pray and fast** – There is nothing like prayer and fasting to defeat the enemy and equip the angels to do battle. Jesus often went to a quiet place to pray and get his marching orders from Father God. He told the disciples to pray and to fast. In fact, in one case (Mark 9:14-29 KJV) the disciples were unsuccessful in casting a demon out of a boy. Jesus entered the picture and when the disciples asked why they were unable to cast out the demon (when it had worked previously), Jesus told them *"This kind can come forth by nothing, but by prayer and fasting"*. If we are to be his true disciples, we should pray and fast as well.

3. **Put on the armor** – Go through the action of putting on the armor of God every day (Ephesians 6:13-17). Put on the helmet of salvation to protect your mind from the attacks of the enemy. Put on the breastplate of righteousness to protect your heart and emotions. Put on the belt of truth, so you will always be girded up by the truth of the Word of God. Put on the shoes of peace, so you will walk in that peace that surpasses all understanding and everyone around you will also feel the peace. Take up the shield of faith to ward off the fiery darts and arrows of the enemy and take up the Sword of the Spirit, the Word of God, to fight off the enemies lies. If it was good enough for Jesus when He was tempted by the devil in the wilderness, it's certainly good enough for us. If you've ever wondered

why the armor has nothing for the backside, it's because God is our rear guard (Isaiah 52:12). The fact is that He's all around us and His favor is like a force field (shield) around us at all times (Psalm 5:12).

4. **Worship** – As we discussed earlier, there are several examples in the Old Testament where God instructed the Israelites to put worshippers in front of the army. Worship draws the powerful and mighty Spirit of God to do battle for you. Where the Spirit of the Lord is, there is freedom – freedom from fear and freedom from harm – no weapon formed against you will prevail or prosper (Isaiah 54:17).

5. **Loose the finances necessary to do battle** – Help plant new churches and ministries; fund missionaries here in the U.S. and abroad; and take care of the poor, homeless, orphans, and widows.

6. **Share your testimony and the gospel of Jesus** (salvation through faith in Jesus, as Savior) with everyone you meet. Don't worry about what they might think or say. You are saving them from eternity in hell. This life is short, and eternity is long. They will thank you later.

7. **Keep fighting the good fight of faith** until Jesus brings you home. Never, never, never give up!

Remember that Jesus said he would never leave us nor forsake us. He goes with us, through the Holy Spirit, into every daily battle. True disciples of Jesus Christ are never alone! That said, fight with the rest of the army. Jesus sent His disciples out 2x2 and in groups, so do the same. Don't try to be the lone ranger or some kind of hero. Satan loves to separate the sheep from the flock, so he can attempt to devour them. Fight with the army of God (other true disciples). Leviticus 26:8 says:

"Five of you will chase a hundred, and a hundred of you will chase ten thousand, and your enemies will fall by the sword before you."

There is power in numbers and God will multiply that power, which is why you must be part of a church army. By fighting together (not against each other), we can subdue our part of the earth and accomplish God's mission.

When God delivered the Israelites from captivity in Egypt, He told them that He was giving them land – the promised land. When they arrived at and spied out the land, they became afraid of the giants and fortified cities, so they didn't take the land. Instead, because of their disobedience, God made them wander the desert for 40 years until the first generation had died, except for Joshua and Caleb (the only spies who brought back a good report). Joshua then led the second-generation Israelites in and took possession of the land God had promised to them 40 years earlier.

We, Christians, are a lot like the Israelites, as we've been wandering around the desert for over 2,000 years. Jesus defeated satan on the cross and returned authority back to man. He intended for us to be fruitful by multiplying true disciples, and to subdue the earth. Unfortunately, we haven't done a very good job of either and so the earth is still chaotic, and Jesus is still waiting.

Once again, Jesus is calling His true disciples to take the land. To subdue and transform the earth into a place that looks more like heaven. You have your calling and your battle plan, so get to work transforming yourself and your part of the world.

END NOTE

1. https://ptv.org/devotional/how-do-angels-help-us

Discussion for Chapter 14: Invading

1. Talk about the armor of God and how to utilize it in everyday life.

2. Discuss how you have been fruitful and multiplied for the Kingdom of God.

3. Share your thoughts about angels and any angel stories.

4. Commit to an invasion plan and share it with your group.

Chapter Fifteen

✝

Now

A t the writing of this book, I feel so blessed to have many amazing ministry stories and yet, I know that I'm not done and am waiting for my next tour of duty. For the last nine years, I've been assisting pastors in the growth of their church and yet in April (2016) the Lord made it clear that I was to be back in full-time vocational ministry.

My expectation was that it would happen immediately, so I prayed and worshipped for hours every day and as God led, I contacted pastors of larger churches and directors of large ministries to see if there was an open door for a seasoned veteran of the trenches. Many doors closed, and a few opened briefly. Some have future possibilities and I'm excited to see what God is going to do with me.

I recognize that His timing is always different than mine, so I know, when it's His time, God will open the right door. In the meantime, I'm not letting any grass grow under my feet. I've completed a master's degree in Christian Leadership from Ascend International University. I also co-founded a ministry for men struggling with sexual sin, called Revive40 (Revive40.com). There is an estimated 40 million Christian men in the United States struggling with sexual purity. It's truly an elephant in the sanctuary that no one wants to talk about. Well, we are talking about it with churches and at men's conferences. In the near future we're hoping to launch an internet training system.

Finally, I created an internet ministry called True Disciple (www.TrueDisciple.info). This ministry resulted from this book. God told me to write my "true disciple" story and as I did, He gave me direction to start the internet ministry. I believe strongly that God is tired of seeing His children sitting in church services and not doing what He said to do – preach the gospel and make disciples, teaching them all that Jesus taught, take care of the poor, orphans and widows.

Still Growing

Karen and I also continue to take classes and attend seminars and conferences. Recently, at one of these conferences, we received a strong prophetic word from a recognized and reliable prophet, that we were to go to Israel. We prayed and received confirmation from the Lord and so we took our first trip to the Holy Land. It was an amazing experience to see and walk where Jesus and his true disciples walked, healed, and delivered people. We know we received impartations for this next season and are excited about what the Lord has in mind.

That ministry trip connected us with the host ministry, David Herzog Ministries. That lead to our involvement in an epic Christian event, Awaken2020, at Arizona State's Sun Devil stadium. We believe that God used this event to begin the awaking process in Arizona and throughout the U.S.

Walking with Jesus, as a true disciple is exciting and rewarding. It's my hope and prayer that this book and my true disciple story will inspire and motivate you to get out from behind the security of the church walls and begin doing what God told his disciples to do – preach the gospel and make disciples.

Invest time every day in the scriptures and prayer to seek God for your calling. It may be that you are called to minister at work by introducing Jesus to your co-workers or perhaps start a lunch time Bible study. Maybe you are called to invent something or start a business that will generate funds you can give to your church, local and international ministries or missionaries. Perhaps God wants you to write and publish a book. He might even want you to start a ministry.

Your Passions

For a moment, think about what you are passionate about? That passion is God-given. Are you passionate about the lost and making sure they are saved? How about the homeless and hungry? Children in the foster care system? Single moms? The elderly? Sex trafficking? Taking the gospel to other countries? Maybe you are called to take the gospel into schools as a teacher or administrator? Could He be calling you into politics, as we definitely need more of God in that realm? Do you feel drawn to arts or entertainment? God will use your passion to lead you to your calling. Once God reveals this calling, step into action and watch what He does through you.

It doesn't matter how old or young you are. Your education and experience levels don't matter. What matters is your willingness to serve. It's been said many times that God isn't looking for the qualified, He's looking for those who are available. Make yourself available to God and let Him lead you into His glorious plan for your life. Just like the original true disciples, you could be a world changer!

www.ingramcontent.com/pod-product-compliance
Lightning Source LLC
Chambersburg PA
CBHW071218090426
42736CB00014B/2882